i

HOT DAME ON A COLD SLAB

Film Noir
Murders No. 2

MARLENE PARDO PELLICER

This book is classified as historical non-fiction. Although it is drawn from history based on research which at times was sourced from oral tradition and the writers' memory, it contains actual historical people, places and photos some minor events could not be documented fully and may be fictitious.

DEDICATION

This book is dedicated to my husband Henry. During a year of extreme changes, some by choice and others forced upon us, he served as my rock, and I was his. We forged bonds that can only be produced by overcoming obstacles together. Through it all, he accommodated those times I would stare off into space and not pay attention, because he knew I was percolating future stories in my head. And to those who accompanied us on our journey. No one got left behind, neither the dogs, birds nor chickens; they are still underfoot and as noisy as ever.

ABOUT THE AUTHOR

Marlene is a native Miamian and has been writing since 1971, (on a manual typewriter when she was eleven years old).

Amid a year of upheaval she relocated to a small town in North Florida with a population that barely exceeds 5,000.

She is the founder of *Miami Ghost Chronicles*, and a paranormal researcher since the 1990s. She is also the producer, host and narrator of *Stories of the Supernatural, Nightshade Diary* and *Supernatural StoryTime* podcast series, and the blog author of *Stranger Than Fiction Stories*.

Marlene lives with her husband Henry (AKA Official Sandwich Maker for Starving Authors) on a small piece of land shaded by Spanish-moss draped live oaks that could easily be the setting for a southern gothic story. Their entourage of animals colors the landscape, with noise and movement. And all is well.

If you'd like to receive my newsletter announcing updates on new books and requests for ideas, please sign up on my website.

www.MarlenePardo.com

OTHER BOOKS BY MARLENE

FICTION

Sibyl Universe

The Dead Cast No Shadow: A Sibyl Novella No. 2 (2020)

The Path to Purgatory: Book 2 of the Sibyl Chronicles (2020)

Diabolique: A Sibyl Novella (2019)

Walker Between the Worlds: Book 1 of the Sibyl Chronicles (2019)

Winter Shade Stories

I've Come for My Girl and Two Other Dark Tales

(Winter Shade Stories Book 1) (2020)

NON-FICTION

Haunted History of the Old West's Wicked Ladies & The Bad Hombres They Loved (2017)

The Lady in the Blue Kimono: Film Noir Murders (2018)

Supernatural Safety: A Paranormal DIY Guide (2018)

NOTABLE LINES FROM FILM NOIR MOVIES

"Prisons are bulging with dummies who wonder how they got there." (The Big Heat)

"He was a ladykiller. But don't get any ideas– I ain't no lady." (Nocturne)

"I wouldn't give you the skin off a grape." (Kiss of Death).

"I haven't lived a good life. I've been bad, worse than you can know." "You know that's good, because if you actually were as innocent as you pretend to be, we'd never get anywhere." (The Maltese Falcon).

"When your head says one thing and your whole life says another, your head always loses." (Key Largo)

"One way or another, we all work for our vice." (The Asphalt Jungle)

"Personally, I don't like a girlfriend to have a husband. If she'll fool a husband, I figure, she'll fool me." (The Lady from Shanghai)

"Oh, well, you're about as romantic as a pair of handcuffs." (The Big Heat)

TABLE OF CONTENTS

CONFESSION FOR A CUP OF COFFEE

NEW YORK, DECEMBER 1923

In a dank moist cell a man sat with closed eyes on a grubby cot. His name was Frank Ranold Benner, born May 15, 1897, itinerant cook and thief. Earlier that day he confessed to the murder of several women in different cities; a serial killer, decades before the term was used by law enforcement. A slight smile creased his cheeks when he remembered the face of the detective who urged him to confess. Hunger and thirst gnawed his insides, and for once he felt satisfied he answered that wretched call of self destruction when he said, "Maybe it was the war that put such ideas in my head. I get wild, like a maniac. Give me something to eat, a cup of coffee, and I'll tell the whole story, I want to get it off my chest. I know I've done wrong, but I can't help it."

NEW YORK, 1920

A woman hurried down the sidewalk as a cold February wind whipped around a fashionable building at 72 West 83rd Street, near Central Park West. She came to the

1

apartment where she lodged, and was surprised to find the door unlocked. Inside a phonograph kept playing jazz music, and it puzzled her why it played so loud. Her heart thudding hard in her chest she followed a trail of blood sprayed against the wall of a hallway leading to a bedroom. Her hand trembled when she pushed the door opened, and then she knew why the tinny music was left uncomfortably loud.

No doubt they silenced the screams of Ream Constance Hoxie, 17, who knelt as if in prayer by the bed, her head rested upon her folded arms. The bed sheets were crimson with blood and her brains.

The Hoxie family moved from Connecticut only two months before. They decided to sublet some of their rooms, and police suspected a man who applied to stay at one of the rooms was the murderer. He was described to be about thirty-five years old, medium build, black mustache and hair, with a swarthy complexion.

Fingerprints and a vague description were the only clues the police were given to apprehend the killer.

Her father and stepmother were visiting a sick relative in New Orleans, and left their teenage daughter home with only the company of the female lodger.

An autopsy found she was raped, and then killed by numerous blows on the back and side of her head with a hammer.

Police arrested several men on suspicion they were the murderer, only to release them when they established an alibi for their whereabouts when the crime was committed.

Robert Hoxie, Ream's father was no stranger to tragedy and heartbreak. In 1907, his 8-years-old son Ralph was killed by an automobile. A year later, his wife Virginia "Jennie" Hoxie, a sculptress gave birth to another boy. They named this child Ralph also.

All was good for the Hoxie family until 1916, when his wife Jennie, 46, died. Now his daughter was lost to him as well.

Like all murder investigations, in the effort to find the culprit, a family's dirty laundry is unearthed as well. Within only a few days of Ream's murder, Robert Hoxie and his second wife, Marie were questioned by the police because it turned out Ralph Hoxie, the 12-year-old brother to the dead girl was turned over to the care of Protestant Big Brothers only seven months before. The Society for the Prevention of Cruelty to Children investigated the family and reported the boy was being treated cruelly by his father and stepmother. Were they the loving parents they claimed to be?

The days passed and Ream was laid to rest in Evergreen Cemetery in New Haven, Connecticut, where her mother and brother lay in their graves.

Marie Hoxie, the stepmother was a concert hall singer who frequently took Ream with her when she performed in Coney Island. Police wondered if perhaps the murderer spotted the girl there when she accompanied Mrs. Hoxie, and found a way to follow her home.

The police also looked for a connection to the murder of Mary Elizabeth Riddell, a 17-year-old girl found killed in a vacant lot near her home at 1839 Briggs Avenue, Queens, NY. This crime was committed almost a year before, and like Ream she had been beaten to death.

The leads evaporated and the cases became cold, but perhaps not as cold as the blood running through the veins of a killer who still stalked women in New York.

MANHATTAN, OCTOBER 11, 1923

A lodging house at 64 W. 97th Street was the scene where Estelle Phillips, 38, was strangled to death. Described as a spinster, she worked as a saleswoman at Saks & Co. for fourteen years. She didn't receive any male callers, and lived a quiet life on the top floor in a $6 per week hall bedroom. She'd occupied the room for six years.

Her friend, Katherine also roomed there and found the body lying across the bed. Estelle was wearing a light undershirt and bloomers which was torn, and blood stained the sheets underneath. Around her neck a white towel was knotted and twisted, but the blue marks of fingers indicated the true cause of death.

Katherine later described to police she awoke a little after midnight, when a strange noise came from the landing outside her door. She peered out and saw a man who rented the room between Estelle and her, starting down the stairs. He carried an Army overcoat and two suitcases. She thought it odd he should leave at such an unusual hour and watched him from a window. He caught a surface car at the intersection of 97th Street and Columbus Avenue.

The landlord, Richard Barry, told police the man moved in only a week before. He gave his name as Frank Collins and he worked as a chef at the Reconstruction Hospital located at 100th Street and Central Park West.

When the police followed up at the hospital they found he was hired on October 4, and before then he worked for a short time in the kitchen at Ellis Island.

After Estelle's murder, a description of the suspect was sent to other jurisdictions. The Philadelphia police said a man answering his description was wanted for the murder of a woman in their city.

A few days later, May Mitchell, 30, a nurse who worked at the Home for Consumptives in Chestnut Hill, Pennsylvania was nearly beaten to death by a man she met for a date. Did the suspect return to his old stomping grounds?

Christmas passed when police received a tip from the Belmont Employment Agency at 841 6th Avenue in Manhattan. They said a man matching the description of the suspect was in their office applying for a job as a chef. They recognized him as the same person they obtained employment for at the Reconstruction Hospital before.

The police hurried over and arrested a man who identified himself as Frank Collins. He denied any knowledge of the murder, but admitted to rooming at the lodging house. He said he served 30 days in the Federal Prison in Washington D.C. but refused to describe the nature of his crime.

Eventually Frank Benner alias Frank Collins made a full confession.

Benner said after killing Estelle Phillips he fled to Philadelphia and lived at the Edward Hotel. He used the name of Frank Clemens, and gained employment at the Shipley School in Bryn Mawr. After stealing money from one of the students he got a job at Chestnut Hill hospital where he met May Mitchell. He admitted to attacking her with a broken bottle, and beating her with his fists.

Benner said he was 26 years old, single and the son of a church worker. He was a stocky man with strong arms decorated with mermaid tattoos.

He told police, "I was a good boy until I came out of the army. I've shifted for myself since I was 8 years old, when my father died. I was in the army 3 ½ years with the 50th infantry, as a company cook."

He went back to the site of Estelle Phillips' murder and reenacted it for them. Mr. Barry the landlord identified him as the same man who abandoned his room right after the murder.

Benner said to police, "Few women liked me, and Miss Phillips was like all the rest. I knew this, though she didn't speak to me while I was in the rooming house."

His prior arrests were tied to burglary charges, and frequently he gained employment at different hospitals as a cook. He also worked on steamships running to Australia.

Between jobs, he visited his mother Carrie Androvette who lived on Long Island. His father Edward E. Benner died in 1906. His stepfather William Androvette died only a few months before in June, 1923.

They questioned him about the death of Ream Hoxie. He told them he was serving a stint in prison for larceny under the name of Thomas J. Bert when the murder occurred. The police verified he was not arrested in Washington until two months after Ream was killed.

Benner's mother said he was deeply affected by the death of his wife in 1919, only four months after their marriage.

Ralph Hohman, married to his sister Edna told police he believed Frank was mentally unbalanced.

On January 5, 1924, Frank Benner was indicted by the Grand Jury with murder for the slaying of Estelle Phillips. He was remanded to the Tombs Prison without bail.

In March, Benner pled guilty to murder in the second degree and separately assault in the first degree against his wife Josephine which he committed in January 1923, when they lived at 335 E. 17th St. New York.

This assault charge, which must have been verified, brings into question his mother's claim he was affected by his wife's death in 1919. Was this another wife?

With this plea he escaped the death penalty. A few days after being convicted by a jury, Judge Mancuso sentenced him "to not less than five years and not more than ten years on a charge of assault, and also from twenty years to life imprisonment on a charge of murder", to be served at Sing Sing Prison.

In 1930, he was serving time at Clinton State Prison and in 1940 at Great Meadow Prison. He was 47 years old, and he fades from records from this point onward. Whether he died behind bars or was granted parole cannot be verified one way or the other.

Was Frank Benner pressed for the names of other women he killed? This was never ascertained. Perhaps the prosecutors were content they could prove their case with the murder of Estelle Phillips.

Three years after Ream's murder a letter was sent to a local New York newspaper, where the writer said he knew the identification of the killer. He described where he hit her with a 10-inch Stillson wrench, and added further details, "About ten months after the murder the man started for Des Moines and stopped at Chicago where his body was found in a back lot on the west side of town, with his head battered in by the handle of an ax." Was this true? The question remained unanswered.

The murders of Ream Hoxie and Mary Elizabeth Riddell remained unsolved.

Frank Benner

Frank Benner being led into court c.1923

Source - New York World

8

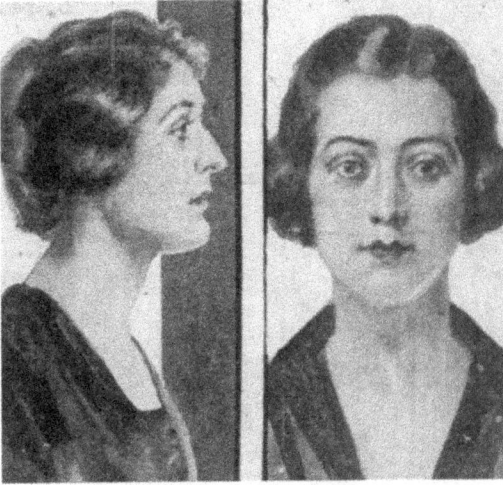

Estelle Phillips (above)
Police removing her body from the apartment
c.1923
Source - New York World

The unsolved murders of
Mary Elizabeth Riddel
and Ream Hoxie (below)
were revisited when
Estelle Phillips was
killed. Were they victims
of the same perpetrator?
c.1923

Source - New York World

Mary Elizabeth Riddell

The newspapers revived the unsolved murder of Ream Hoxie everytime a woman was killed in her home by an unknown assailant

Source - New York World

Right—Ream's stepmother, Mrs. Robert Hoxie.

Left—Ream's mother, Virginia Ream Hoxie.

House Where Strangler Killed Woman in Her Room

House at 64 W. 97th st., Manhattan, where strangler murdered Miss Estelle Phillips. Arrow points to her room.

Cross indicates Hoxie apartment at 72 W. 89th St., where Ream Hoxie was murdered in February, 1920.

The places were Estelle Phillips & Ream Hoxie were killed were very similar
Source - New York World

WHAT HAPPENED TO WILLA?

MORRIS, ILLINOIS 1929

Mrs. Joseph Hunt along with her husband enjoyed the soon ending summer days as they motored across Illinois on Highway 7. They lived in Detroit but were vacationing in the area. Their car bumped on the road, and they pulled over on the side. As her husband labored to change a flat tire, Mrs. Hunt saw a new burlap bag tied up with a wire. The bulky contour of it attracted her curiosity. She stifled a scream when they discovered a woman's nude body in a sitting position inside it. A 40-pound rock on top of her held her in place.

Examination of the remains indicated it was preserved for over a month before being dumped on the side of the road. Even more mysterious was that no wound or cause of death could be found by the Grundy County coroner. There were no bruises, lacerations or bullet wounds. He sent the organs to Chicago for analysis in order to find any traces of poison. Other physicians who examined the body were puzzled as well, but the fact that it appeared someone was trying to dispose of the corpse indicated foul play. The sack was dumped only a short time before it was discovered since the grass underneath it was still fresh.

The victim's age was estimated to be 45 to 60 years. She weighed about 110 pounds and measured 5 feet 3 inches. Her gray hair had never been bobbed and her two front upper teeth were gold-filled.

Most interesting, it appeared once the body was placed inside the burlap bag it was kept in a refrigerated room before rigor mortis developed. There was clay on the victim's skin, which the authorities guessed meant the murderer first meant to bury her, then changed his mind and put her inside the sack.

The police started referring to the murder as a "perfect crime" where a non-traceable form of gas or poison appeared to be used. They hoped the results from the tissue sample would provide an answer.

The police searched the reports of missing women but none fit her description.

On September 6, 1929, three days after the discovery, Mr. Richard Shea came to the coroner's office to view the decomposed remains, with hopes to end the mystery of his wife's disappearance. Then he received word from her she was alive and well, and living in Washington D.C. Thus another lead hit a dead end.

The police found two boys from Morris who said they talked to a party of three motorists, parked at the spot where the body was found only a few hours before. Inside the car was an elderly man accompanied by a younger man in his early twenties. Hiding in the back seat was a young woman. The boys thought the car broke down and offered assistance. A gruff refusal answered their attempt at a good deed. The boys instead of leaving stayed talking to the party. They learned they were from Chicago, but nothing more than this.

Clues petered out, and they even questioned a local hunter Nicholas Carvallo who frequented the area close to where the gunny sack was found. A few hours later they released him.

The days ticked by and then another unusual discovery seemed to point in a queer direction as to what happened to the unnamed, dead woman.

LOS ANGELES, CALIFORNIA 1929

On October 7, 1929, newspapers wrote about the discovery of Willa Rhoads (Rhodes), 16, who was considered a "high priestess" of a strange cult in Los Angeles. A sealed, cedar casket was found underneath the floor of her foster parent's home located in Venice. The police unearthed a pit measuring four feet square by six feet deep, saturated with seawater. Inside her coffin the girl reposed with knees drawn up to her chest and her hands crossed. There was suspicion she was sacrificed as part of a ritual. Next to the girl's casket, another one contained seven dead puppies. Later the police were to learn they represented the seven tones of Gabriel's trumpet which would hail the girl's resurrection.

The Rhoads adopted Willa in Portland, Oregon when she was two years old. They told police she died on New Year's Day, 1925, from an ulcerated tooth. They preserved her with ice and spices for a year hoping to resurrect her through the cult's power. They admitted to not summoning a doctor to attend the dying girl.

An examination of the body failed to produce proof that Willa met a violent end, but the police suspected she did not die of natural causes.

It all started when Clifford Dabney, a wealthy oil operator from the area filed a complaint of grand theft against the leaders of the group. Police brought in Rev. May Otis Blackburn known as "Her Heavenly Highness, Queen May", and her daughter Ruth Weiland Rizzio.

After placing the complaint he sought constant police protection, claiming his life was in danger once he exposed them.

Dabney served as president of the cult from 1925 to 1927, and used the title "Hereafter" and "Now". He claimed fear for his life is what kept him in the position. During those years he paid $4,000 to purchase 600 "sacred" chickens which could only be imported from Europe and a "sacrificial" truck for the sect.

Clifford wasn't the only one asked to "sacrifice" their vehicle; other devotees were instructed to leave their automobiles to rust on the compound's grounds to signal their loyalty. Animal sacrifices were also thought to take place there.

Mrs. Blackburn and her daughter convinced him to give them money for building a printing plant, which would allow them to produce a book revealing the location of rich mines and jewel troves.

According to the women, these were instructions given by Angel Gabriel. They told him the solar system threatened his family if he didn't give the money to publish the book titled, "The Sixth Seal". The construction of the printing plant never took place. In total he gave them $40,000, and a 164 acre property in Simi Valley, that later the press dubbed Harmony Hamlet.

Eventually more members filed theft charges against May Blackburn. In total they gave her approximately $50,000.

A week later Los Angeles investigators sought the burial grounds of the Divine Order of the Royal Arm of the Great Eleven. This was the cult the Rhoads belonged to, and based on a tip given by a former member their cemetery was located at Big Bear Lake.

Missing members of the cult were being sought. Two were men who at one time were married to Ruth Weiland; Edgar "Jack" Rickenbaugh in 1919, and Samuel Rizzio in 1924. Sam disappeared after a fight with Ruth.

Others were Addie McGuffin, Katherine Voltz, Barbara Jeffrey, Floyd Steffen, his wife Phoebe and their two daughters.

Other deaths which came to the authorities' attention was Frances Turner, 30, "reported to have been baked in a stone oven" to cure her of a strange blood malady.

Another mysterious death under investigation involved Harlene Satoris, age 20. The day before police set out to find the cult's graveyard, they received a letter from Harlene's parents, who lived in Oregon. They were as mystified as the police about the death of their daughter. They said it occurred when she was at the cult camp in the Santa Susana Hills. Her death certificate was signed several days after she died. She suffered from medical and mental issues, and once released from an asylum in Oregon, she ended up a devotee of May Otis Blackburn.

Mr. Satoris stated in the letter, "Our daughter did not join any cult. She went to California in the hopes that she would be restored to health from a nervous breakdown and weakness of the heart. She passed away from heart disease and had the services of a regular doctor, who resides in Moorpark. We have a deed to a lot in Ivy Lawn Cemetery, Ventura where she is buried. I spent some time investigating the authenticity of the "Sixth Seal" (the book which Mrs. Blackburn asserts was dictated to her by an angel and will explain the mysteries of life and death) but came away mystified. We did not live with the so called colony, but had our own cabin away from the rest while trying to get information as to when the printing plant would be completed."

Pending the outcome of the coroner's report, Willa's parents along with May Otis Blackburn and her daughter Ruth Wieland-Rizzio were held in custody facing fifteen counts of grand theft.

After the hearing, police released Ruth Weiland and charged her mother with 12 counts.

Ruth in a weird departure from reality complained the six hundred chickens only laid six eggs per day.

The following day the homicide squad released Mr. and Mrs. Rhoads, claiming they could find no proof to refute their claim that Willa died from an infected tooth. The county coroner's tests failed to find a trace of poison.

Mrs. Rhoads demanded the return of Willa's body as well the seven dogs. The request was denied since the girl's remains were still being tested, and the dogs would be cremated.

May Blackburn testified she was aware the couple kept Willa's body on ice for sixteen months and then buried it. There were daily ice deliveries made to the house to stop decomposition from setting in. The body was moved during three residence changes. She denied she promised the girl could be resurrected.

A former member, Jennie Toy, told the district attorney she met Mrs. Blackburn in Oregon, in 1922. They showed her a worn out bible, maps and "other stuff". She and her husband moved into the Blackburn's home where her husband was prohibited from working. She was a stout woman who was given the names of "Speed" and "Swiftness." She confirmed they all carried out "Queen May's" weird instructions because they feared for their lives.

A Beverly Hills automobile dealer testified a girl cultist was forced from his car at gunpoint by cult members after she told him to she wanted to escape and was in fear of her life.

Merritt Wooddell known as "King of Peace" described how he was shot in the heel by instructions of Queen May when she issued a "divine order" and not by mistake as claimed by other members.

Walter and Jennie "Grandmother" Blackburn were brought in to testify. Jennie was May's mother, and she married Walter Blackburn in 1913 in Oregon. It was through them May met her husband Ward Blackburn, who was Walter's son. He was 20 years younger than her, and the couple married on January 11, 1924.

Jennie, 65, was known in the cult as "Queen of the Scale". She told authorities how she was chained willingly to her bed for two months in a house on Wilshire Boulevard. She did this to establish a "point" or to complete a "religious constellation". According to the older woman, "The Angel Gabriel finally released me, that is spiritually. My concord of the musical scales made it necessary for me to remain where I was, at my 'point' until the Angel Gabriel told 'Mother', my daughter, to release me."

At the same time Ward Blackburn known as "King of the North Star of the Grand Central Point" acted as "weatherman". He told authorities, "When we lived on Wilshire Boulevard, I counted all the cars and made a report to my wife. When we moved into the Susanna Hills I counted the trains. When the weather was clear, well, it was clear, and I made a record of it. When it rained I put out a coffee can and measured the water when the storm was over." He was an unusual character with 5-inch nails who sported a "Chinese mandarin's mustache".

These orders were carried out at the behest of "Mother Blackburn" who claimed she received instructions from the Angel Gabriel.

Walter Blackburn, 71, told of marrying Jennie, after his wife died. The newspapers noted, "May Otis Blackburn, 48, and her husband, Ward 29, are stepbrother and stepsister." Despite the fact they were unrelated it brought to light the age difference between them and cast an incestuous pall over the union.

During those days, the forty remaining members of the cult moved to the hill camp. It was evident they expected to be summoned by the district attorney. Perhaps they anticipated his next line of investigation would be the disappearance of Sammie Rizzio after he allegedly struck his wife who was considered a "messenger".

Instead of explaining what happened to her husband, Ruth Rizzio told authorities his true surname was Scarletta but he did not use it because his family fled Chicago to avoid trouble.

Frankie Rizzio, Sammie's brother told police shortly after his brother's disappearance, Ruth produced a letter supposedly written by her husband explaining why he left. He suspected it was a forgery, and he offered to work as a chauffeur for the cult in order to investigate his brother's fate. Several days later, Sammie's traveling bag was found, despite the story given he took his belongings with him when he left.

The Rizzios threatened to go to the police, but May Otis Blackburn probably knew they hid their own sordid past they feared would be revived. Sam served nine month as a juvenile for altering checks, and his father had been wanted in connection to a triple murder. It appeared he was involved with the Black Hand in Chicago.

Before the arrest of May Blackburn and her daughter, Frank Rizzio noticed the disappearance of Willa Rhoads. He was told she went to Altadena to teach. Other members said she headed east to get married. None told him she died and was buried under her parent's home.

The Rizzio's threats were never acted upon, but four year after their son's disappearance they got their chance to air their misgivings to the DA, when May and Ruth were arrested.

Two letters allegedly written by Sammie Rizzio were reviewed by handwriting analysts. One had the same misspelling as Ruth's writing, and one sent to his mother was written by a right handed person, and Sam was left handed.

Among those questioned was a cult member who agreed to provide information if they hid her identity. She led the authorities to the sect's cemetery.

She was a pharmacist and said Mrs. Blackburn came to her to obtain poison. May said the Angel Gabriel wanted her to kill Sam with a poison "which cannot be detected in the body of a drowned man". When the woman expressed doubts, she was told he would be resurrected after the publication of the Sixth Seal. The pharmacist told police that despite May's reassurance she gave her a vial of colored water.

The authorities wondered if the pharmacist lied in order to protect herself from blame. She said May obtained chloroform, and tests made on the dogs buried next to Willa Rhoads confirmed this chemical was used on them

In 1925, in Topanga Canyon, Sam Rizzio deep in the grip of the cult danced like a dervish in sand sprinkled with a powerful poison. He did this ten times in order "to rid himself of another belief that prevented him from accepting his concord in the Great Eleven." His belief in Catholicism, according to May Blackburn was the barrier.

On October 10th, May claimed Angel Michael visited her. She described him as "a handsome man with long black hair."

She declared, "All these trials and tribulations are just to test our loyalty to the faith. Michael exhorted Ruth and me to keep steadfast and we will. He was only with us a little while but he explained all the troubles would be cleared, and then he smiled and disappeared."

Based on Dabney Clifford's suit, the Ventura County deputies seized the "Lord's Furniture Set" from the sect's Santa Susana headquarters which was valued at $20,000.

Another piece of the puzzle regarding the cult's activities came when George Jeffrey wired police to help find his missing daughter who he claimed his divorced wife took into the sect without permission of the Oregon courts.

Another man, Carl Osborne, once engaged to Ruth Rizzio told police she'd been a dance hall girl, but the disturbing part of his story involved the disappearance of a woman known only as Mrs. McGuffin. He said she'd been missing since he joined the cult several years before, and was the widow of an oil operator living in the area.

The investigation confirmed that some members were deeper in the operation of the cult than others. Gale Conde who acted as a secretary for May Blackburn copied down the messages she received while in trance, which were how the contents of the Sixth Seal manuscript were produced.

Finally during the trial, Mr. and Mrs. Rhoads confessed that in November 1924, May Blackburn brought them down from Portland. She told them Willa was one of eleven queens who would rule the world from Hollywood. Upon the girl's arrival she was gifted with seven puppies, the same ones sacrificed next to her. On Christmas Day she developed a tooth infection that without medical attention killed her on New Year's Day.

The promised day of Willa's resurrection came and went, and then the cult leader told her parents she'd been "sacrificed to save the world". This statement coupled together with the invitation of her parents to come to Los Angeles, the gift of the dogs, her sudden illness and her death on the portentous date of New Year's Day suggested these events were planned. However they were only circumstantial and the district attorney could not prove Willa was murdered.

Was there a connection between Willa and Sam's death? They were very close in age, and both disappeared within months of each other.

During the proceedings it became known Mrs. Rhoads had an adult daughter, Mrs. Richter, wife of a San Francisco attorney. When police arrived to question them, they were told the couple was spending two weeks in New York. Mrs. Richter said she had not seen her mother for several years, but they corresponded regularly.

Had someone tipped them off so they would be conveniently out of town and unable to answer questions?

More people came forward to speak of the cult's activities. They described ecstatic dancing in the nude over the graves of two slaughtered mules. This occurred out in the desert at Death Valley by the instruction of Mae Otis Blackburn to "represent the passing from death to eternal life."

During the day the cult members worked at tomato packing sheds, and turned over their paychecks to Queen May.

The main building at the colony was called the "The Church of the Divine Science of Joshua, the Branch of the Headstone of the Corner". Flora Dingman a member cared for a two-year-old child known as Baby Jehovah, who was expected to become the second Messiah. A 500 pound gilded "Christ Chair" with the head of a dog was made to await his arrival.

On October 22, Willa was buried at Woodlawn Cemetery. The autopsy surgeon reported the girl died of natural causes.

By Halloween, May Blackburn posted a $10,000 bail and was set free. In December, twenty-six persons from Ventura County were presented with subpoenas to testify in court.

The trial lasted six weeks and in March 1930, she was found guilty of eight counts of grand theft. She was sentenced to one to ten years on each count to be run concurrently at San Quentin Penitentiary.

In June the cult's household goods were sold at auction. A gold-leafed bedroom set supposed to have cost $6,000 sold for only a few hundred dollars.

In December, 1931, the California Supreme Court granted May Otis Blackburn a new trial. They held the first trial invalid because testimony dealing with activities of the Great Eleven cult was admitted, when it should have been confined to the book, The Sixth Seal alone.

In May 1932, the state dropped the charges against May Otis Blackburn and by the end of the year, she was once again presiding as priestess over the cult. They positioned a guard at the entrance to their Santa Susana compound, and the sect members were also armed.

Eventually they relocated to the Lake Tahoe area.

In 1935, 3,400 acres, which included the area once used by the Church of Divine Science of Joshua was offered to Ventura County as the site for a new penitentiary. Abandoned buildings still dotted the area, and in 1939 the compound burned to the ground.

William and Martha Rhoads, Willa's adoptive parents both passed away in 1944.

May Otis Blackburn died on June 17, 1951, in Los Angeles from heart disease. Records indicate her birth name varied from Matilda May Otis to Matilda Jane Otis. In the 1920 census she lived with her daughter Ruth, and her son-in-law Edgar Rickenbaugh in Los Angeles. She listed herself as May O. Holmes.

In 1919, Ruth married Edgar Rickenbaugh. On May 24, 1924 she married Samuel Rizzio, 18, at the First Christian Church, Santa Ana.

Strangely enough the bride's birth date kept changing on the marriage records, making her younger than her husbands, when in truth she was a few years older than each of them.

Ruth Angeline Rickenbaugh Rizzio Williams née Weiland , her name at the moment of her death, passed way in December 19, 1978, in Sacramento.

Ward Sitton Blackburn, her stepfather, died on June 24, 1975, in Los Angeles.

Addie McGuffin who was reported as missing when she belonged to the group, rejoined in the 1930s. Supposedly she was tasked with secreting away the copy of the Sixth Seal. She died in 1946.

The seed of what became known as the Blackburn Cult sprang not from mystic insight but from desperation after a failed film career. Mother and daughter starred and produced the film A Nugget in the Rough (1917) while living in Portland, Oregon. They moved to Los Angeles in 1918, but four years later Ruth supported them working as a "taxi dancer", many of who also prostituted themselves.

In retrospect, May Blackburn may not have predicted Dabney Clifford would go to the police, but she knew eventually someone else would, or authorities would question where she got her money from.

In February 1925, four years before the discovery of Willa's grave, at a construction site in Topanga Canyon a metal box was plowed up. It contained a dozen love letters between Oregon lumber king Fremont Everett, a married man, and May Otis Blackburn. The letters detailed an affair that reached its height from 1917 to 1918.

Another letter stated, "That for value received I have given you notes amounting to $25, - 400 and I solemnly promise and agree not to sell, bargain or convey the bulk of my property until I have paid you, or settled to your entire satisfaction". In total according to the letters, May received $100,000 from him.

Inside the box were several snapshots the district attorney presumed were May and Everett. It was apparent he was averse to having his picture taken, and tried to hide his face, while the woman made sure her identity was unmistakable. There were copies of the photographs inside as well.

The wording of the letters written by Everett plainly indicated a great deal of infatuation with the object of his affection.

Freemont Everett denied he ever wrote the "love letters" to May Otis Weiland (the name she used then). He said he knew her only through business deals when purchasing property from her which is why some were written on his company stationary. Mr. Everett was a small-framed, 60-year old man, and his associates vouched he was not the type to get mixed up in a sordid love triangle.

When May was asked about the contents of the small box, she admitted to the affair, and said she buried the box after Fremont refused to leave his wife, and then dug it up herself.

Was this a publicity stunt concocted by May to explain where her money was coming from? Some believed May did have an affair with Fremont, but did so intentionally in order to blackmail him, and also falsify some of the letters. The language was stilted much like Sam's letters. There were also repeated references to numerology, a major concern of the cult.

There were other circumstantial incidents pointing to darker deeds than defrauding gullible followers of money.

In 1928, May took nine of the group to the desolate desert landscape of Stovepipe Wells in Death Valley. Later police investigated to see if Sam's body was disposed of inside one of the wells. A few months later, May instructed Willa's father to bury a large trunk at Big Bear Lake. She never told him what was inside. The police tried to find the trunk and verify if Sam Rizzio was inside but they could not locate it.

Sam Rizzio's whereabouts remained unknown, and his family never heard from him again. If killed, is he buried somewhere in Topanga Canyon, Big Bear or in a well at Death Valley?

Like him, the dead woman found freshly thawed inside a gunny sack and left by Highway 7, in Morris, Illinois, remained a mystery. A month after the discovery of the victim, Sheriff Jones began an inquiry into the possibility a cult was responsible. He looked to the similarities between his case and those of Willa Rhoads. The crime was never solved, nor her identity established. More than likely she was buried in a pauper's grave in a local cemetery.

The nude body of a woman was found frozen inside a gunny sack weighed down with a 40 lb. rock along Highway 7 in Illinois c.1929

Willa Rhoads died New Year's Eve 1924, she was discovered
in a secret tomb under her adoptive parent's home in 1929.
Source - The Sacramento Union

The Rhoads house where Willa's tomb
was discovered (above)
Police unearthed a separate coffin
that held 7 puppies

A police detective dug
through a hole in the bedroom
floor of the Rhoads' home in Venice.

Ward Sitton
Blackburn (L)
was 20 years
younger than
his wife,
Rev. May Otis
Blackburn

Ruth Weiland Rizzio with her missing husband Sam Rizzio (L)

Ruth dressed in an exotic outfit (below)

Rev. Blackburn, her daughter
& other members (above)
Female members of the Order at its temple
on Wilshire Blvd, c. Oct. 7, 1929 (below)

Cult Probe Bares Weird Story

Flora Dingman & Baby Jehovah. The Christ Chair made of gold with a dog head was made for him.

(L) Merritt Wooddell AKA The King of Peace holds The Light of God c.1929

"GREAT ELEVEN" PRINCIPALS

Walter and Jennie "Grandmother" Blackburn, above, newest figures in the cult investigation. Below, Ward Sitton Blackburn, "Little Dipper" of the cult.

Walter & Jennie Blackburn (above)
William & Martha Rhoads (below)
c.1929 *(Source - The Sacramento Union)*

A cult temple that eventually became derelict by 1932
(Source - The Sacramento Union)

CLIFFORD R. DABNEY

Clifford Dabney (L) placed the complaint against Rev. Blackburn that started the investigation into the cult's activity

Topanga Canyon (below) where the cult held rituals, and where a search was made for Sam Rizzio's body.

GERTRUDE'S
LOVER

YORK COUNTY, PENNSYLVANIA NOVEMBER 1927

Sunset streaked the horizon on a chilly autumn evening when Gertrude Rudy, 16, met in secret with someone who occupied her thoughts night and day.

Unknown to her, Paul Long, known in the area as "Dummy" Long saw Gertrude and a companion get off a street car. He was employed at the nearby Spring Hill Brick Factory and he hung around the depot. He made a habit of watching couples who met for a tryst in the area of the Maryland & Pennsylvania railroad track. Well at least, that's the story he told police later.

Within a few hours Gertrude's body was discovered on the track by a "canned heat" addict named Warren Dupes (Dupuis). He was an occasional farmhand, who shucked corn and was headed to the brick plant where he was in the habit of sleeping, even though he actually lived at a hobo camp close by known as Hollywood.

Later other farmhands who walked along the tracks to their home found the corpse, and moved it off the tracks until police arrived.

39

Police believed her body had been left on the track with hopes a train would run it over and disguise the true cause of death. However the evening train had rolled through by the time the murder was committed.

The morning following the discovery of Gertrude's body, Paul Long who was deaf and mute, along with an interpreter came to the police to tell them what he saw. He took them to the scene where the footprints of the fleeing man tracked into a nearby wheat field.

He described that about 8 p.m. he saw a man wearing a hunting jacket and carrying a shot gun on his shoulder walk east on the M & P tracks with Gertrude Rudy. He'd seen the girl before and knew who she was.

Staying hidden, he followed them as they walked some distance, then the man lifted the gun, pointed it at her and then the flash of the discharge illuminated the darkness. Then he clubbed Gertrude with the butt end of his weapon. She fell backward and the man ran off. Paul made it understood that if he saw the man again he could identify him.

Afterward, Amos Herrmann the District Attorney, discounted Long's story, since it was determined he had a child's mind and he suspected the man made up many of the details in order to have a moment in the limelight.

Inside the girl's pocket was a small vial of perfume wrapped in Christmas paper, with a note that read, "to Neil Stough from Gertrude Rudy, 844 East King Street". This was how the police identified her.

Neil was her 16-year-old sweetheart, and he was questioned, but then released. The police wondered if the girl used him to cover for her illicit romance with possibly an older, married man.

Another man questioned by police was Luther Luckenbaugh, 49, who lived next door with his wife Anna at

846 King Street. Anna was Gertrude's aunt. He was released as well, after denying any type of intimate relationship with the teenager.

To add to the urgency of discovering the culprit it turned out the girl was a niece of Chief of Police A. H. Stevens.

The post-mortem was performed by Dr. Robert Lee Ellis, he said, "the girl had a fractured skull, concussion of the brain, cuts on the face and that a hole evidently made by a shotgun was in her left side. Her heart and lung had been penetrated by the shot."

The doctor confirmed the girl was pregnant, and the police wondered if her killer did away with her in order to avoid a scandal.

On November 14, the day of Gertrude's funeral and burial at Mt. Rose Cemetery, the York County Commissioners offered a reward of $300 for the arrest and conviction of her killer.

The girl lived with her grandmother, father and several siblings. Her mother died in 1922, but by then she'd divorced Gertrude's father and married another man.

A day later the police received a tip from the proprietor of an inn who told detectives of a vagrant who acted suspiciously. The man was in his late 20s, about 5'9" tall and weighing about 160 pounds. He came to the inn asking for food. He carried a double-barrel shotgun which he offered to sell for $3. He told the innkeeper he was tired of carrying it around. The man appeared nervous and evasive. He also had a deep cut running from his left ear to his mouth. He wore a gray suit and a brown, slouch hat. The innkeeper went to find food for him since the man complained of only eating a pumpkin the day before. When he returned the man was gone.

The man was later sighted at the Cumberland Valley railroad station near William's Grove asking about the train schedule. He was told the next passenger trains were bound for Winchester, West Virginia and the other towards Harrisburg. He commented he didn't want to go to Harrisburg, and then asked about the movement of freight trains.

By the following day the unnamed man had become a suspect the police wanted to question. They followed him to woods near Brandtville in Cumberland County. The obvious description of the man was the cut across his face.

Others said he hung out in the area since the prior summer when he worked with a party collecting reed for basket making.

Another day passed and the authorities were unable to catch up to the suspect. A farmer living towards Dillsburg told police he believed someone had gone inside an abandoned blacksmith shop across from his house. They inspected the property and found someone had indeed spent the night there.

As hope for finding the hungry man who visited the inn evaporated, the police confirmed that a few days prior to her death Gertrude had visited a York physician due to her pregnancy. Luther Luckenbaugh, accompanied her. He told police the girl wanted him to get something that would end the pregnancy, but he refused her. She told him she was ready to kill herself if word of her condition got out. When the doctor asked who the baby's father was, she stated it was Neal Stough.

The local residents were desperate to find Gertrude's murderer, as she was the fourth victim to die in the county due to foul play.

Samuel Thompson, 28, didn't understand how intense the manhunt was for the perpetrator until he joked with a neighbor that he was the one that murdered Gertrude. He found himself arrested by the detectives assigned to the case the same day, and taken to city hall for questioning by the district attorney. He finally convinced the authorities he was only joking, and he was released.

Thanksgiving came and went and no other leads came to light about the murder. A coroner's jury was convened, and their verdict was that "Miss Rudy came to her death from a gunshot wound through her heart, and injuries to her head, by someone unknown to the jury at this time."

Anna Boyer, Gertrude's friend testified the girl knew she was pregnant and that Neil Stough was responsible. She told Anna, "I want to talk to him alone."

Anna tried to help her friend by arranging a meeting at her home. For one week prior to her death, Gertrude waited for Neil, but he failed to appear. She also told Anna the floor lady at the plant where she worked knew of her condition. When Anna tried to cheer her up, Gertrude said, "If you'd be me, you'd do anything."

The year ended and authorities were no closer to identifying, much less arresting who killed Gertrude. The district attorney paid for the bed of a nearby dam to be dragged in hopes the murder weapon had been disposed of there. But nothing was found. The man hired to do the work, told police someone had watched him stealthfully from behind some bushes while he worked.

By April 1928, the newspapers reported that "nothing new" had emerged concerning the Rudy murder. The message was clear. A murderer proved to be more cunning than any of the police detectives assigned to the case.

Detective Myers diagrammed the victim's movements on the night she was killed. She went west on Princess Street from her house to the home of Elwood Einsig, who she stopped to converse with. She crossed the street, traveling east on Princess Street, then re-crossed the street and was seen by Mrs. Silar, who was well acquainted with the girl as she walked eastbound on the 900 block of East Princess Street. That was the last seen of Gertrude that evening until her corpse was discovered on the tracks.

In August 1928, Neal Stough was arrested, and then released after questioning. At first he denied having a sexual relationship with Gertrude, but finally admitted they were intimate, but that he didn't know who killed her.

Later that month Paul Long, the deaf mute man who told of witnessing the murder of Gertrude Rudy was arrested and placed on probation for one year after entering a plea of guilty to a charge of open lewdness.

Anyone who was connected to the Rudy murder made the papers, even if it was on an unrelated matter.

As the anniversary of Gertrude's murder neared, the only story appearing in the newspapers was the total lack of results by the police department in solving the crime.

In December 1928, John Blymire was questioned about the Rudy murder. He was a suspect in the witchcraft murder of Nelson Rehmeyer. He admitted to knowing the girl. He lived near her and worked at the same factory. He also attended her funeral.

Police searched his room in hopes of finding some type of correspondence between him and Gertrude. Their thought was that perhaps in desperation she turned to witchcraft in order to avoid the shame of being an unwed mother. This avenue of investigation also hit a dead end.

To make up for the months were no progress was made on the case, in December 1928, police found a second suspect besides Blymire. Sarah E. Shank of Marietta, 17, was taken into custody indirectly as a result of the pow-wow murder case. She stated that she knew who killed Gertrude Rudy. Police questioned her, and she told them she overheard Theodore Latshaw, 21, confess to the murder. He was picked up for questioning immediately.

Latchaw, had married the month before Gertrude was killed. He said he knew who she was, but had nothing else to do with her. Eventually police released him when he admitted he lied about being the killer. Sarah Shank, for her troubles was sent to a local girl's reform school.

In April 1929, newspapers reported on the death of John Shiley. He was described as a World War I veteran who became addicted to dope. He was committed to the county hospital to treat his addiction. They placed him in isolation, and then soon after he disappeared. Two days later two junk dealers rummaging around a dump on the Herr farm came across his body. The corpse had lain in a field for about three days.

One of the doctors, who treated him at the county hospital, came to the scene and explained that when Shiley came in for treatment, he swallowed several "dope tablets" which he took from his pocket. Due to his actions they transferred him to the insane department, and then the doctor brought him back to the isolation unit. He escaped by walking out the back door. He had only $1, which in those days was enough to buy an "ample quantity of dope and canned heat."

According to the doctor, Shiley's problem started when he was still in the military, and he received treatment at the Perryville and League Island hospitals. The hospital once spoke to Shiley's brother living in Virginia who told them, he was "not interested".

Farmer Herr told police he sometimes let strangers sleep in his barn, and had occasion to speak to Shiley, who told him he had a mother and a wife living in Middletown. Family disturbance had caused him to take to the road.

At that point, authorities decided that if family members could not be found to take the body he would be interred in Potter's Field.

However, it appeared the Mr. Shiley had a problem with the truth, starting with his identity. Once York police arrived, it was found his true name was Warren Dupes, 36. He was not a veteran at all, but suffered from addiction to drugs and alcohol. This contributed to his death which was determined to be from exposure.

He had been one of the first who found Gertrude's body on the tracks. After being questioned he was released.

Dupes married Virgie Bryans in 1916, and they had four children who lived at Royalton. He grew up in the area, and left home five years before, abandoning his family entirely. Instead of burial in a pauper's grave they sent him back to his family, where he was interred in the Middletown Cemetery.

Many wondered if perhaps Warren Dupes killed Gertrude, which is why he was one of the first to find her, but in truth they knew it was a futile effort to close a case, where the criminal killed a pregnant, young girl and outsmarted all of them.

By 1929, mention of Gertrude Rudy drew in newspaper readers, and everything surrounding her was publicized, all except the most sensational headline, which would be the story about the apprehension of her killer.

On August 23, her grandmother Cathrine, 70, a widow died from a heart attack. Her husband William had died earlier that year on January 1. She followed her unfortunate granddaughter to the grave less than two years after her murder.

As the second anniversary of Gertrude's murder approached the district attorney, Amos Herrmann, reached out to a remote possibility that the arrest of Harry Malaga in Boston might lead to the resolution of the murder. Mr. Malaga was being questioned about the slaying several weeks before of Samuel Reinstein (Rheinstein), a New York furrier and racketeer. He'd been shot to death in a local hotel.

The slim thread he hoped tied the cases together was the recent discovery by federal and state agents of a white slave ring operating in York and other Pennsylvania counties. Mr. Herrmann felt the local murder might link up with 50 other cases involving the traffic of these young girls. The investigation found 4 York girls were victims of the ring. The D.A. wanted Malaga questioned as to his whereabouts on the night of Gertrude's murder or whether he knew her.

While the Samuel Rheinstein murder case bubbled in Boston, witnesses in the case were guarded from "gangland guns". Federal officials began an intensive effort to run to earth a "master mind" believed to be complicit in the 50 murders laid at the door of the "white slave" ring that extended from Massachusetts into Pennsylvania. The fear was that the witnesses would end up like Gertrude. This put a new spin on the girl's murder altogether. Perhaps she hadn't been killed by a married suitor afraid of a scandal, and instead because she became a burden to a white slave ring.

When Henry Malaga was questioned about Gertrude he refused to answer any questions.

The "white slave king" was believed to be headquartered in Pennsylvania, between Bethlehem and Easton, and once operated at least 50 establishments that extended through Pennsylvania, New Jersey, New York, Connecticut, Massachusetts and Rhode Island.

The authorities' main witness in the Rheinstein case was his girlfriend Elizabeth "Betty" Martin, who the Department of Justice took into protective custody.

Days before the stock market crash in October, 1929, the federal investigation found that a thousand girls were furnished by a vice ring which operated between Boston, York and Easton, Pennsylvania. Their business also extended into smaller cities in New England. The authorities estimated the gigantic system earned several million dollars a year. Of interest to York County's district attorney was that a large number of young women brought to the northeast came from York County.

The federal authorities were set to question a girl who had long been connected to the ring and was a very close friend of Gertrude Rudy. She was considered a chief figure in the case, and it was because of her which led to the killing of Rheinstein. Inspector Donovan who oversaw the federal efforts was apparently very distrustful of those surrounding the investigation, and said, "He had good reasons for not having this young woman taken into custody."

At least 40 automobiles were traced since they were believed to have been used to transport the girls around.

The kingpin of the operation was not only implicated in cleaning up millions of dollars and prostituting young girls, there were allegations of transporting vast amount of narcotics and the wholesale murder of scores of men and women. They described this unnamed criminal as the "emperor of vice."

Most troubling of all was the probable extent of official corruption into several communities in New England. Ironically the prevalent corruption existed among minor county officials who were accepting graft for a number of years.

"Practically all of the important evidence gathered by the small army of investigators in this section of the country, has for police reasons, been carefully guarded. Attorney Tarr explained, 'We cannot give out facts or disclose in any way the results of our investigations. This is a huge affair and before any action is taken in any section we intend to have every bit of evidence connecting every person who has had any dealings of any nature with this ring. We are trusting to no one. I doubt if the public or press will ever learn of evidences gathered in this case until the grand juries have listened to it in detail. One must realize that hundreds of men and women from the leaders down are involved in murder and every known crime on the calendar'".

The original investigation was triggered when numerous raids were completed in order to close out every house of ill fame. When the girls were arrested and questioned, it came to light how young they were. The girls taken from Pennsylvania, New Jersey and New York numbered in the hundreds.

Unsurprisingly the ring was able to hire the best legal teams to defend their members. Those arrested including Harry Malaga, were bailed out with bonds the in tens of thousands of dollars provided by one of the leading bailing companies of the country.

The ring hired a former Assistant United States District Attorney, whose retainer fee was not less than $50,000. The accused faced charges of violating liquor and prohibition laws.

The murders committed not only involved young girls; there were deaths as a result of disputes between proprietors and operators, between white slave rings and gangs, hijacking each other prostitutes, and of course there were those "taken for a ride" because they squealed or knew too much.

The girls were trafficked from one circuit to another in order to provide fresh faces to regular patrons.

The task force involved in the investigation discovered a large, previously abandoned farm on the outskirts of White River, Vermont, used as the headquarters for the same rings. The house was bought in 1927, by a man living in Germantown, Pennsylvania.

Not only were girls from the northeast taken there, but others from Quebec, were held for "sorting and distribution to the industrial centers of southern New England." The girls in the New England brothels were from Pennsylvania while the girls taken to road houses which dotted the eastern section of New England were from New England and Quebec.

Drugs were used to "break in" the girls, and the actual farmhouse was secured through the efforts of young women who were once inmates there.

The ring did not operate any brothels in Vermont, New Hampshire or Maine. It was a complicated investigation, in which it turned out to be impossible to determine if Gertrude was a victim of this crime syndicate.

Gertrude Rudy's name disappeared from the newspapers until it would surface in later years, either to point out that the police failed to solve the crime, or when a murderer was caught nearby and efforts were made to tie him to the case.

Ultimately the Rudy case was never solved. The person responsible or the reason behind it remained unknown. Perhaps Gertrude's allure or value ended once she became pregnant or worse if she threatened to tell everything she knew, and despite the best efforts of the District Attorney to find the guilty party, she was silenced to make sure she never would.

Gertrude Rudy's body found on the railroad tracks
Source - The North East Sun

YORK GIRL, 18, SLAIN; BODY FOUND ON R.R.

Skull Shattered With Gun Shot, Corpse Dragged To Railroad

**Gertrude Rudy (above)
York County Railroad Depot**
Source - The North East Sun

Death of Warren Dupes once suspected in Gertrude's murder c.1929

Source - The North East Sun

RELATIVES BURY TRAMP IN RUDY MURDER CASE

The man who discovered the body of Gertrude Rudy, murdered in York on November 11, 1927, and who was found dead in a dump near Millersville, Lancaster county, was Warren Dupes. He was known in the neighborhood where his body was found as John Shiley. He was 36 years of age. He had been absent from his home in Royalton, near Middletown, for five years.

The man was born and reared in Royalton and left home five years ago, leaving a wife and several children behind. Later he entered the Lancaster county home in Lancaster for treatment for his health. Five days ago he disappeared from the home and Saturday was found dead from exposure by two men who were walking in a field near Millersville.

The body was taken to Roth's undertaking establishment, Middletown, and funeral services were held at 2 o'clock this afternoon with the Rev. R. E. Morgan, pastor of the Royalton United Brethren church, officiating. Burial was in the Middletown cemetery.

Later there was suspicion that Gertrude Rudy's murder was tied to organized crime in the Northeast c.1929
Source - The North East Sun

FEDERAL AGENTS FEAR UNDERWORLD WILL KILL GIRLS GIVING EVIDENCE

AUTHORITIES SEEK "MASTER MIND" RESPONSIBLE FOR 50 MURDERS IN OPERATION OF RESORTS.

Boston, Oct. 1 (INS).—While men and women witnesses held in connection with the Samuel Rheinstein murder were guarded today from gangland's guns, federal officials began an intensive campaign to run to earth a "master mind" suspected of perpetrating the fifty murders that had been laid by federal investigators at the door of the "white slave" ring in the east and which extends to the mining region of Pennsylvania.

Officials were fearful that the witnesses might share the same fate of Miss Gertrude Rudy, who was slain Nov. 11, 1927, on the outskirts of York, Pa.

THE SOCIAL DISEASE

NEW YORK, JUNE 8, 1896

The night was still warm despite the hour of 1 a.m. Three shots rang out, and two policemen standing at Division Street and Chatham Square ran towards the noise. In front of Kelly's Saloon stood a man with a revolver in his hand; when he saw them he started to run, tripping over the man he just shot.

They gave chase and finally captured him. Returning to the scene of the crime, a crowd informed them the victim was James O'Brien, 35. After pulling him from the gutter, an ambulance was carting him off to the Hudson Street Hospital with a bullet in his lung.

The shooter was John W. Hahne, 21. Both men were heard arguing about money before the shots sounded out. An old sailor who witnessed the altercation said Hahne had "fired a shot through his own hat and a second in the air." The police believed he did it to make it appear he had been shot at first.

Strangely enough neither one gave any information to the police about their background or the reason for their dispute, only claiming they just arrived from Chicago.

However, police recognized them as "old-time crooks and former pals".

Hahne formerly kept a saloon at 66 Pike Street, and O'Brien lived there with him.

Two days later O'Brien was still alive, but refused to tell police who shot him. Police held onto Hahne waiting to see if they would end up charging him with murder. According to the doctors though, it seemed O'Brien would recover, which he did. John W. Hahne was released but this would not be the last time his name appeared in the newspapers connected to a crime.

OMAHA, NEBRASKA JANUARY 1925

At the foot of the basement stairs, John Warren Hahne and a plumber who accompanied him found his wife's body splayed grotesquely in a pool of blood. Her body was gashed in several areas. A doctor was called, who in turn summoned the police.

The instruments of Mae Hahne's death were close by. A hammer and hatchet with clots of blood and strands of hair was hung over her husband's work bench. Work clothes with blood on the suspenders were also found by police.

Mae had more than a dozen foot long wounds on her head, and the knuckles on her right hand were broken when she tried to defend herself.

When presented with the circumstances of the woman's death, a coroner's jury recommended that her husband be held on a charge of first degree murder. Hahne, a contractor and real estate dealer, denied any involvement in his wife's death, claiming he last saw her alive before he left for work in the morning.

The police considered robbery as the motive. Two rings valued at $1000 each were missing, but strangely two diamond earrings were left behind.

Mae Schaeffer Hahne was a highly educated woman. A graduate from the University of Wisconsin and the University of Chicago, she owned a dry cleaning business with her first husband Hiram Bennett. The marriage ended in divorce and she married John Hahne, a widower, December 1915 in San Francisco.

His first wife Alice committed suicide on November 14, 1911, in the bedroom of their Bronx home.

Within two days of Mae's murder, John Warren Hahne was being referred to as a "wealthy apartment house owner and former New York gangster."

Perhaps anticipating the defense attorney's strategy, the prosecutor filed insanity charges against the 48 year old. If the insanity board found him to be sane then first degree murder charges would be applied and he would seek the death penalty.

According to Dr. G. Alexander Young, alienist, it appeared that Hahne suffered from paresis, a social disease he contracted years before which ate away the upper part of his jaw and nose. It also caused softening of his brain. A "social disease" was the euphemism used in those years to avoid the term syphilis. In its later stages it caused inflammation of the brain, progressive dementia and paralysis.

The county attorney Henry Beal insisted that despite Hahne's diagnosis he planned the killing of his wife and carried it out at the breakfast table. It was alleged he attempted to wash away all the blood in the dining room, but large splotches were found in the carpet.

A post-mortem examination found Mae's stomach was empty, which led them to believe her killer struck before she ate breakfast. Rigor mortis had just set in when she was found a little after 2 p.m.

Dirty dishes left by John to establish an alibi, testified to the fact that after killing his spouse he sat down to eat the food she prepared for them.

The authorities believed he dealt her a blow at the breakfast table, and then dragged the body down the stairs. He struck her several times with a hatchet, hammer and iron bar. She suffered 24 hatchet wounds in the skull.

Despite the evidence provided by the examination, Hahne presented an air-tight alibi for his whereabouts until 10 a.m.

In New York, police now looked with questioning eyes at the death of Alice V. Hahne, his first wife, now dead thirteen years of an apparent suicide. Detectives were planning to question neighbors in the Bronx neighborhood where the couple lived for several years.

Alice (Allice) Hahne, according to police records, was found lying dead on her bedroom floor, with a vial of poison next to her. Neighbors claimed the couple had quarreled before her death, but Hahne denied he had even been in the house.

Despite an intense investigation at the time, it was closed as a suicide. Shortly afterward, Hahne left New York and traveled out west.

Review of county records by the Omaha authorities confirmed that John Hahne had tried to kill his wife Mae before. The district court disclosed he'd been incarcerated twice in the state hospital for the insane; the last time on October 24, 1919. Mrs. Hahne stated in her complaint she feared her husband would "harm her".

One time he knocked her to the ground and poured gasoline over her. About to light a match to her clothing, a stranger intervened and saved her. A year later, it was Mae herself which petitioned for his release stating she wanted him close to her.

A leak in the plumbing under the bathroom floor was found by the authorities, which confirmed Hahne's claim his wife wanted him to bring a plumber to fix it.

Police questioned neighbors. One was 12-year-old Margaret Hedges, she told them she came to the Hahne home at 10:15 and 11:30 a.m., and then again at 1:30 without anyone coming to answer the door.

Another neighbor, Della Lightfoot stated that Hahne suffered from hallucinations that his wife was complicit in a conspiracy to take his life.

Hahne's own sister, Sylvia Beats testified her brother believed he would be killed by his wife, and that in turn she would be killed by a gang headed by a relative who sought control of his properties.

On January 10, police discovered the dead woman's missing jewels which were secreted in a compartment of a drawer. This dispelled the motive that she was killed for her jewels which were estimated to be worth $3,500.

A week later, Hahne appeared before an insanity commission, where he cried openly still protesting his innocence. The small room was packed with 300 onlookers. Within a few days, he was adjudged insane and committed to the state hospital for treatment. One of those who accompanied him to the hospital was a person many didn't know existed. His name was F. Welton Hahne, 28, the accused's son by his first wife Alice. He was a mining prospector living in Montana.

By mid-February most of Hahne's apartments were empty and people refused to live in them because of the murder. The house where Mae Hahne was killed sat vacant since the tragedy.

A milk man making an early morning round rushed from one of the apartment buildings located on Omaha's south side. He waved down policemen and with a trembling voice told them he heard groans and moans coming from inside. They searched the property and found the place was untenanted. Was it the spirit of the slain wife haunting her killer's property?

By the end of March, Mae's relatives were contesting her will which left a $25,000 estate to her husband. They claimed that her will was worthless because it reciprocated one made by Hahne at the same time in 1916, when he was mentally ill. They claimed he was not capable of giving her his estate in return.

In a strange twist to the Hahne murder, Thomas Bronder, the plumber who accompanied Mr. Hahne and was present at the discovery of his wife's body suffered a complete breakdown because of the incident. Eventually he was committed to the state asylum.

In April 1927, he escaped from the Douglas county hospital and was recaptured with the help of his brother-in-law who found him armed with a 3-foot pipe. The doctors in charge of his case decided to remand him to the hospital in Norfolk this time. The reason was they feared he would cross paths with J. Warren Hahne who was responsible for his mental condition.

Money seemed destined to come Hahne through his wife's death when in July 1925, a judge sustained that a $5,000 insurance policy issued against Mae Hahne would be payable to him despite his insanity.

In 1928, Hahne's friends were working to obtain his release from the state hospital. County Attorney Henry Beal wrote a letter to the commission claiming a delegation of people living in the vicinity of the killer's home urged him to make a protest against his release. Apparently they took heed of his letter, and in 1930, John Warren Hahne was still a patient at the Lincoln State Hospital for the Insane. He disappeared from public records and what became of him is unknown, however considering his age and diagnosis he most probably died as a patient in the asylum.

Apartment Houses Owned By Hahne Said Haunted By His Slain Wife's Spirit

OMAHA, Feb. 18.—Does the departed spirit of Mrs. Mae B. Hahne, murdered wife of J. Warren Hane haunt the apartment houses owned by her husband?

Residents on the south side, where the houses are located seem to think it does. It was learned today, when a milk man, making his early morning rounds rushed from one of the building and in a trembling voice told police officers he had heard groans and moans emanating from it.

An investigation by police showed that the place was not tenanted. They failed to hear the strange sounds reported by the milk man.

Investigation disclosed further that most of the Hahne apartments are now empty, people refusing to live in them because of the murder.

The house in which the woman was found brutally murdered has been vacant since the tragedy, M. N. Graham, administrator of Hahne's estate admitting he can find no one brave enough to live in it.

Graham ridicules the idea that ghosts are inhabiting the Hahne apartments but admits that many tenants have left and that their places have not been filled.

Hahne, who was accused by a coroner's jury of murdering his wife was later declared insane and is confined in the state asylum at Lincoln.

**John and Mae Hahne at their wedding
in San Francisco c.1915**
Source - Omaha Daily Bee

Downtown Omaha
c. 1920s

Source - Nebraska State Historical Society

John Warren Hahne
c.1925

Source - Omaha Daily Bee

THE

SECRET

OF

LONESOME PINE

STONY POINT, NY APRIL 15, 1922

At the top of a trail that climbs Cheesecock Mountain near Stony Point, New York is Lonesome Pine. At the foot of the mountain was a place known as the New York State Home for Incorrigibles which opened in 1911. It was an asylum for girls named Letchworth Village.

Clarence Conklin the son of a night watchman at Letchworth went to the top of the lonely mountain to pick berries. It was here he found the skeleton of a girl. Wisps of hair were still attached to the skull where it lay half buried between rocks. Other bones were found wrapped in a newspaper. He told his father, who put the remains in a sack and brought them down.

The officials at Letchworth did not believe she had come from the asylum, despite the fact that the month before seventeen girls escaped from the home. Every week thereafter several girls ran away, and most were never recovered. Even before the discovery of the skeletal remains, many wondered what was the fate of the "half-witted girls" once they left the grounds of Letchworth Village.

In a nearby cave, blankets from the asylum were found. They were bloodstained, and the initials of the cottage they belonged to had been torn out. This was how approximately 130 buildings that sat on nearly 2,400 acres were identified.

Three years before, another girl's body was found. Her skull was crushed. Only a week before her death, she'd been observed living with a man who stayed in a tumbledown cabin at the foot of Lonesome Pine. Once the murder was discovered the man disappeared from the area.

Now once again there had been another girl killed. The coroner estimated she had been no more than 19 years old. She wore her hair bobbed, and her skull had been crushed by a small jagged rock, left beside her body. None of her clothing could be found.

Mary E. Hamilton head of the New York City Women's Precinct, was the first policewoman to serve in New York City, and she brought in a retired former head of the Bureau of Missing Persons. He reconstructed the battered skull, and three weeks later she was identified by her sisters Katherine Copertino and Rose Doran.

Her name was Lillian White, 24, and indeed she had been staying at Letchworth Village. She measured 4'9" and weighed only 95 pounds. She had brown hair, several teeth missing and adenoids which thickened her voice; she lisped as well. Along with her violent temper she also harbored abnormally passionate affection.

The image was also recognized by Dr. Charles Little the superintendant at Letchworth and two nurses. They said she ran away after being punished for writing a letter to a man. She was last seen on February 13, 1921, and was believed to have fled from New York. What led them to believe this was never explained.

Those who attended Lillian at Letchworth said she was not vicious, but did have an unpredictable personality. It was this characteristic which landed her in Letchworth. Once there, an examination found she was not entirely normal mentally. Before this Lillian had been sent to Bedford Reformatory. She was the youngest of seventeen children, fourteen which died before reaching adolescence. Her mother ended her days in an insane asylum, and her father served prison time, and died two years before from acute paralysis. Since she was two years old Lillian was shuffled from one state home to another.

Once the remains were identified as belonging to Lillian White, the police in Haverstraw believed they knew the name of the man who killed her.

With the revelation of the girl's murder, "stories of crime, depravity and vice" were uncovered about the quiet mountains overlooking the Hudson. They told of shanties used by criminals to hide loot, and along the way spirit away weak-minded patients from Letchworth which housed 1,500 inmates. There were other girls who ran away and were never heard from again.

During the investigation of Lillian's murder it came to light she often escaped at night from Letchworth to meet male attendants of the institution. Before her murder she was involved with a mill worker who had shack nearby.

Authorities observed the trail which led from Letchworth to where the body was found was marked by slashes on the tree trunks as if made with a hatchet. Had this been done to mark a trail for the girls?

Interview with those living in the area told of Letchworth employees that came from a mountain clan, itself a huge family where intermarriages had given all of them the same familial stamp on their features. Scandalous stories came from Haverstraw of trades people and loungers meeting with the girl inmates as well.

A woman reporter disguised herself as a potential employee to gain entrance into the asylum. While waiting for a taxicab, a hotel manager told her, "Expect to work up there? You won't stay very long. No young girls do. It's certainly a terrible place. And they do say all sorts of things happen that never get out. Yes, you'll get a job. They always need people up there. But I'm willing to bet you don't stay."

A taxi driver taking her up to Letchworth commented, "They found the corpse of a baby out in the mountains too."

Within days of the investigate journalist being assigned to work in Cottage J at Letchworth, and her expose being printed as a series in the newspaper, the district attorney dismissed county officials, detective and investigators working on the murder case. This was the price of exposing what was going on at the state run institution.

Prior to this police were looking closely at Joe Crawford an attendant at Letchworth. He'd been reprimanded more than once for paying too much attention to Lillian. He filled a cave on the mountain with rugs and furniture which they suspected he stole from nearby estates. He also built a cement doorway to the interior. Supposedly girl inmates escaped at night and visited him and his friends there.

It appeared that once the investigation into Lillian's murder was uncovering a deep problem at Letchworth, the local authorities withdrew their support and tried to block further inquiries.

Suddenly attempts were made to say the reconstructed skull was not that of Lillian White. The coroner William T. Stahlman examined the skull and said eight teeth were missing and Lillian had only four missing. Then the Rockland County District Attorney Morton Lexow insisted the skeleton was not Lillian. However imitation pearls said to have been worn by the girl were found close to where the skeleton had lain for over a year.

These disclosures also prompted parents of girls staying at Letchworth to inquire into the wellbeing of their daughters, fearing they would end up dead like Lillian White.

Dr. Little the superintendant, in response to the criticism said the trouble started a year ago when he was forced to admit delinquent girls with criminal pasts. He had to receive more than a hundred girls from Randalls Island and Bedford.

In mid-May Joe Crawford, the attendant from Letchworth Village was found in New Jersey. He married Ruby H. Howe a nurse who worked at the asylum back in February, around the time Lillian was last seen alive. On the night of March 14, while attending at a movie show with his wife, he got up from his seat during intermission and never returned.

By the end of May, Lillian's family was demanding an indictment against Joe Crawford, and testimony was to be presented to the Grand Jury the following week. The courts officially declared the bones to be those of Lillian White, and her remains were turned over to her relatives for burial.

In the meantime, they found Ruby Crawford in Maine; however she refused to say where her husband was staying.

A year slipped by and in March 1924, a startling murder theory was presented by Dr. Anna W. Hochfeler, attorney for Lillian's family, about the fate of 11 girls missing from Letchworth Village for the past two years.

The latest were Mary Weissnek and Helen Johnson who disappeared only two weeks before. Their unknown fate led to a demand for a special deputy attorney to prosecute the man that Dr. Hochfelder would accuse of murdering Lillian White.

The law didn't catch up to J. J. Crawford until May, 1925, three years after the discovery of Lillian's remains. By then he was using his real name of Harry A. Kirby, and he was being questioned not about Lillian's murder, but about charges involving the homicide of Aida Hayward and the shooting of her aunt Emma Towns.

According to a story told by Mrs. Towns, "She and her niece returned late at night from Winthrop Village to their cottage on the east shore of Lake Maranacook and as they opened the door, two shots were fired from within. Both bullets struck Mrs. Towns. She fell on a couch in a half-conscious condition and later heard the voice of a man telling Miss Hayward that if she would accompany him on a journey of fifty miles no harm would come to her. She heard Miss Hayward ask: 'But what if my aunt should die?' The man then came over and looked at her as she lay on the couch. Afterward he went upstairs and she heard him speaking of money."

She fainted, and the crackling of flames awakened her. She was alone and the house was on fire. Mrs. Towns, 65, bleeding from bullet wounds on her neck and arm dragged herself from the cottage as the blaze engulfed it.

Within hours over 2,500 people joined in a search for her niece. On May 23, only two miles from where she was kidnapped, Aida Hayward's nude body was discovered hidden between two mattresses on a cot in the locked second story room of a cottage on the shore of Lake Maranacook. She'd been strangled and raped.

Kirby soon became a suspect, since he'd once occupied the cabin where the victim was found. Up to then, the only thing police knew about him was that he was a factory worker, whose wife inherited a small sum shortly before he appeared at the home of Ted Bearce and asked for a room. He said he rented the cottage on the lake belonging to L. Jane Gray but that he "would not stay in the place another night for $1,000." Then he disappeared.

A posse of sixty men along with the state police tracked him down to Newburyport, Massachusetts where he was arrested, but rumors of a mob gathering at the railway station in Portland, urged them to Kennebec County jail in haste. Kirby said he had not killed Aida Hayward but hid her body in the cottage to "protect someone else"; a person who remained unnamed.

Once Kirby's alias became known, as well as where he'd lived, Lillian's family demanded that he be indicted for her death. They were certain he was the former Letchworth attendant known as James Joseph Crawford. Dr. Anna W. Hochfelder former attorney for Lillian's relatives told the newspapers that District Attorney Morton Lexow, "Failed to do his full duty in the White case. If he had been more zealous and had taken the matter seriously instead of as a joke, this second murder might not have been committed."

The inference was unmistakable. Since Lillian had been a poor, slow witted girl that met her tragic end because of a propensity to meet with men, her case never received the attention it should have. However, the murder of Aida Hayward, and the attack on her aunt Emma, both outstanding citizens who lived in a quiet town in Maine, had brought forth decisive action to find the culprit, which it did within days of the crime being committed.

Hochfelder disclosed that back in 1922, Crawford had been traced to Maine, and contact made with his wife Ruby, and all efforts to find him stopped because Lexow refused to bring him back to Rockland County on the plea he lacked funds.

It wasn't only Aida Hayward's murder that could have been avoided if Lexow had acted, but possibly Alexander Buchanan whose body was found in an abandoned cellar hole in Waverley, Massachusetts on the grounds of the McLean Hospital only a month before Aida Hayward's murder.

Buchanan had been waylaid, gagged and his hands were drawn down under his right knee and secured with ropes at the wrists. A new type of Navy gas mask was tightly strapped on his head and face and filled with chloroform. The gag tied behind his head with strings remained inside his mouth. The medical examiner concluded that due to the construction of the mask, chloroform trickled down the breathing nozzles and caused asphyxiation.

During the investigation of this murder it was discovered the victim would occasionally be dropped off on the ground of the School for Feeble Minded at Waverly to meet a young woman. Had Kirby been working there?

In investigating Kirby's past, police believed he was arrested in Queens in 1919 on a charge of burglary. He was then known as Harry or Louis Blunt. He escaped shortly after his arrest.

On June 4, Kirby confessed to the murder of Aida Hayward and the attack against her aunt. He told authorities he was in a "drunken frenzy". He traded the confession for two egg sandwiches and a cup of coffee, to be prepared by his wife, which she did. Another motivator for his confession was his fear of being extradited to New York to stand trial for the murder of Lillian White. If convicted on a murder charge, he could find himself executed with the electric chair. In Maine, the worse he would face was life imprisonment.

During his confession, police observed that he had a sneering sarcastic manner with an ego-centric personality. "He gloried in the yarn he told and his cunning little eyes glittered as he gave the details one by one. At times he laughed and joked about it. He knew he was going to get into the newspapers, a thing he has eagerly sought since his arrest. One thing that helped to make him talk was the fact that he was practically dropped out of the newspapers for days and it bothered him."

Prior to the murder he would rob places in Moseley's Kippewa camps and then pawn his loot in Boston.

Described as a "swarthy little consumptive", he confessed he was familiar with Aida Hayward and her aunt and the location of their cottage. He knew Aida was worth about $30,000. When he stayed at the Gray cottage nearby he would prowl around at night and steal what he could.

He planned only to rob the cottage, kidnap Aida Hayward and extort money from her wealthy family. He knew the two women were in Winthrop to attend entertainment given by members of the Order of the Eastern Star. He estimated when they would arrive home, so he broke in and waited for their arrival.

People in the area came to ask his help to put out the fire he started at the cottage where the women lived. Unknown to them Aida lay dead upstairs.

He accompanied the men, and rendered assistance to put out the fire. While there he expressed his sympathy and told them that whoever did it should be strung up.

Within hours of confessing to the murder in Maine, Kirby attempted to kill himself.

At the beginning of September the Kennebec county grand jury indicted Kirby on the charges of murder, attempted murder and arson. He recanted his confession and pled not guilty when arraigned on the charges, with the exception of the arson charge.

On September 14, he attempted suicide in his cell by cutting a vein in his left wrist with a razor blade. He was discovered still alive by Sheriff Cummings early in the morning, but then died in the afternoon. He left a letter to the sheriff that read, "Have thought the matter over and have decided to sacrifice my life to the state of Maine rather than plead guilty to a brutal and vicious crime of which I am not wholly guilty. If my wife does not claim my body, I should like to have you surrender the same to the Bowdoin College Medical School for purposes of study if they care to claim it."

Apparently he was unaware that the medical school had been closed for several years. The authorities were unable to find his wife, who was said to be staying somewhere in northern Maine.

As he suspected his widow refused to claim his body, so it fell to the state to dispose of his remains. It could not be ascertained how he came by the razor blade he used. He was buried in a pauper's grave in a cemetery in Augusta, Maine cemetery. The only ones present were Evangelist Lawrence C. Greenwood who conducted the services and a few cemetery workmen.

Letchworth was featured in a 1972 documentary titled, *Willowbrook: The Last Great Disgrace*. Geraldo Rivera through a series of investigations visited Letchworth and found that residents there lived in dirty, overcrowded conditions. Reforms did not appear until the end of the 1970s. Letchworth was closed in 1996, and the buildings were abandoned. They fell into decay, many who worked there refused to speak of their experiences.

Lillian White (above) Her likeness was reconstructed from her skeletal remains. Below is her sister, notice likenss

Source - New York World

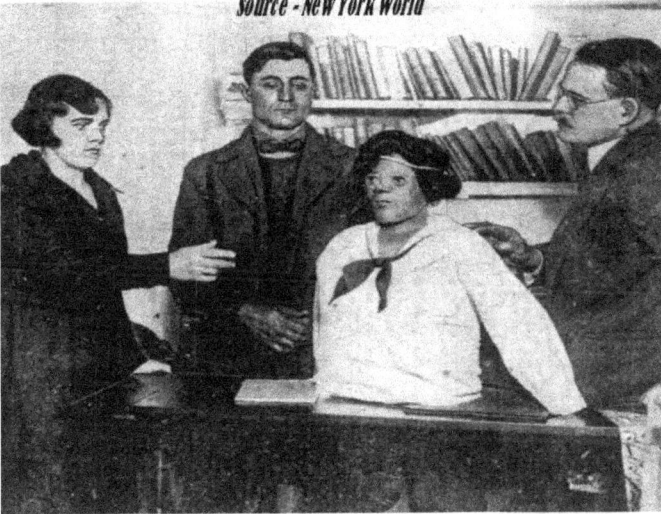

Mary Hamilton, was the first policewoman to serve in
New York City, she spearheaded the effort to reconstruct
the unidentified victim found on Lone Pine

Source - New York World

An investigative journalist posed as a worker at Letchworth Village to report on the conditions the girls lived under

Source - New York World

Ruby Kirby and her daughter Maxine, she refused to cooperate with police in locating her husband after Lillian's murder, and she disappeared when he was arrested for the murder of Aida Hayward
This picture was found in Kirby's wallet when he was arrested.

Source - New York World

Aida Hayward (right) was raped and murdered by Harry Kirby (below). He ended up committing suicide in jail

Source - New York World

Remains of cottage on shore of Lake Maranacook where
Kirby shot Emma Downs (below) then set
fire to the structure
Source - New York World

THE SKELETON UNDER THE SQUAWBUSH

SAN BERNARDINO, CALIFORNIA MAY 1945

John and Clora McMillan with their seven children lived in Bloomington, a small citrus community in San Bernardino County. One day John came to Sheriff Shay with a strange story. His wife Clora had disappeared. She worked at the Army's air depot, and there was no explanation for her disappearance. The sheriff took the report and the months rolled forward. It seemed as if the earth had swallowed Mrs. McMillan up since no trace could be found of her whereabouts.

That changed on Labor Day 1945, when two dove hunters came across a woman's skeleton under a squawbush. She was doubled up, nude and covered with a brown coat. Her heavy, brown hair was hidden by a stocking cap. There was a pair of wedgie shoes nearby. The authorities guessed the body had been placed there before June because the coat

83

was scorched by a brush fire that had swept the area in that month.

The coroner examined the skeletal remains and concluded the woman, age 22 to 35, had been murdered.

The McMillan home was only a mile away, and the sheriff wondered if he finally found the missing Clora.

John McMillan, along with his two oldest children, and his in-laws came to view the remains. They said the teeth were like the missing woman's, as well as her hair. They identified the shoes and cap as hers, but weren't sure about the coat.

One of the children told the sheriff that the night before his mother disappeared he heard her speaking to a man he knew as Blackie, and that she agreed to meet with him in Bloomington.

Blackie, real name Lee J. Webb, was a 21-year-old laborer who was immediately located by police. He lived in a trailer at a camp near the area. The tall, young man said he knew Clora McMillan and that she spent two nights at his trailer. She left because on the second night he struck her.

The police suspected there was more to the story and pressed him to disclose everything. After spending a night in jail he admitted to murdering Mrs. McMillan. He told police, "She threatened to leave, because I had been drinking. I got mad and hit her in the stomach. The last words she said were, 'You've hurt me'. I was scared. I thought she was dead. I put my head down to her chest and her heart wasn't beating. Sure she was dead!"

He borrowed a car and took the body out to the desert and hid it under a squawbush. He led police directly to the place where the skeleton had been found. This along with the confession convinced the sheriff they had the murderer.

The McMillan family along with Clora's parents, Mr. and Mrs. Smock, buried the bones at a Colton cemetery on

September 10. Webb had already admitted to everything once again when he took the stand at a preliminary hearing.

One day after laying their daughter to rest, the Smocks were shocked to receive a long, handwritten letter from Clora postmarked from Lancaster, a town in Los Angeles County. She asked about the children, and explained she left because she couldn't take her husband's drinking. He was 20 years her senior.

On September 17, while Lee Webb was entering a plea of not guilty by reason of insanity, Mrs. McMillan was being arrested. They waited for her when she came to the post office to pick up a letter from her parents.

The police took her back to San Bernardino. She explained to them how she did meet Webb that night at a Bloomington bar, and as he described, she spent two nights with him. Then he told her she had to leave because he found out her husband was looking for her.

She then hitchhiked to El Centro and met Alexander Nelson. The chemistry was instantaneous, and she told the officers, "He was good to me, so we went on to Yuma, Arizona where we were married. He didn't know I was married and had seven children. It isn't his fault. He loves me with everything he has."

She used the name of Evelyn Oleson, and the newlyweds moved to Lancaster. She read about her death and funeral in the newspapers. She thought of her children, and she didn't want them to grieve for her, which is why she sent the letter to her parents.

Now that it was evident that Clora McMillan was not a murder victim, police brought her to meet Lee Webb.

The sheriff asked him, "Do you know this woman?"

"Sure, I know her. Her name is McMillan."

He was sent back to his cell, and he told the sheriff the next morning his lawyer had instructed him not to talk anymore; however he did admit the murder story was not true.

By way of explanation he said, "I just got to talking and couldn't stop."

When he was asked how he knew where the body was found, he replied, "That was just a lucky guess. Mrs. McMillan is safe and I have nothing more to say."

The charges were dismissed, and as he walked out of jail, Clora McMillan walked in to face the charge of bigamy.

The coroner ordered the skeleton exhumed. Enough skin was used from a thumb to use as a print, and the police were hoping this could help identify the woman.

By mid-October, police had brought in at least four suspects, but failed to produce enough evidence for a murder warrant.

Almost two months to the day after John McMillan held a funeral for his wife, he was granted a divorce. The reasons stated were abandonment and her bigamy. He got the automobile and the house, and asked for custody of the children, but the courts had not arrived at a decision. A month later Alexander Nelson asked for an annulment, which might have been moot if indeed the marriage was valid at all.

The only bit of luck Clora got was that the bigamy charges were dropped.

In the meantime, the police were trying to establish the identity of the remains, in hopes they could find who killed her.

They considered the skeleton could belong to Gertrude Gray, 28, an employee at the San Bernardino Army Air Field who had been missing since June 5, when she left for a trip to Enid, Oklahoma. She took a 60 day leave to be with her pregnant sister. Her parents reported her missing, and since then no trace had been found of her.

However police suspected the woman left under the squawbush had been dead longer.

Deputies then looked into the disappearance of Helen Crail, 28, who disappeared on March 3, during a trip to her dentist's office. Her height and hair color corresponded with the mystery skeleton, however the teeth were different.

Lee "Blackie" Webb on the other hand couldn't seem to stay out of trouble. He was arrested for receiving stolen goods and violating probation. He'd been arrested the prior December for indecent exposure. While in jail, he spun a new story. He said he went to a party at the home of Jack Keen on April 17. While there, he witnessed Jack beat a woman to death, and then he was forced to help him take the body to Bloomington.

Strangely enough his story was corroborated by another guest at the party. Waitress Beulah Foster, 36, testified at a coroner's inquest that Webb and Keen had been in a fight that resulted in a woman's death. She said the woman was "an expectant mother, they called her, 'Babe'".

Webb said that Keen, along with Beulah, two other women and a man went to Keen's house to have some drinks. He said he went to the bathroom because the alcohol made him sick. When he came out everyone was gone except for a nude woman on the sofa. He didn't know who she was and asked Keen what happened.

Keen said, "I've killed her."

When Webb tried to leave, he threatened to kill him too. Keen then felt for a pulse and she was dead. They loaded the body up and took it out to the desert, depositing it under the squawbush where it was found in September.

According to Beulah Foster, the argument between the woman and Keen stemmed from her accusation that he was the father of her baby. He denied it. She said, both Keen and Webb hit the woman. An ambulance was called, however the men took the body to the car before their arrival. The pair was gone for about an hour. When they returned Keen threatened her she'd better keep her mouth shut.

The police confirmed with the ambulance service their arrival at Keen's address, but they said the house was dark. The driver returned later with police and the party had resumed, however everyone denied that any injury had occurred.

Beulah Foster said she told the Colton police about the woman being beaten and killed. She described her as being, "brown-haired, slightly over five feet tall and dressed in a skirt and blouse and short length coat." A coat of the same description was found on the remains.

When Jack Keen was brought in by police, the tough-looking cowboy came in wearing his boots. He hailed from Oklahoma where he operated horse stables and a riding academy. For the last 12 years he did construction work around Southern California. He denied Webb's story.

The district attorney said the state would not issue a murder complaint against Jack J. Keen based on the accusation of Lee "Blackie" Webb and Beulah Foster alone. Keen's credibility had been damaged when he confessed to the murder of Clora McMillan which turned out to be totally false.

He doubted Beulah's testimony because she admitted during questioning that during the party she was very drunk and that she "didn't remember much".

R.L. "Jack" Wilcox, 45, a day laborer was being held in county jail on vagrancy charges. Beulah said she went to the party with him, but she knew him as George Budd. Jack Keen identified him as one of the men at party. When Keen was asked he said, "I couldn't say yes or no". Wilcox denied knowing any of them, and that he didn't attend the party.

Beulah didn't get her happy ever after. In January, 1946, she married Thomas Lashlee and by November of that year he was granted a divorce to end his marriage to her.

In life, the bad luck that haunted the mysterious lady killed and left in the desert, persisted in death. Sheriff Emmett Shay who was in charge of the investigation directed his attention to a gruesome find on January 1, 1946 of a dismembered woman tossed down a ravine on the Rim of the World highway.

The department's efforts were now focused on this new case.

There were none to find the answer to the questions as to who was Babe and what happened to her? Whose skeleton was found in the desert under the squawbush? Did Lee "Blackie" Webb or Jack Keen get away with cold-blooded murder?

Clora McMillan, mother of 7 disappeared & was presumed dead until she turned up alive, with a new name and married to another man

Source - Hemet News

Lee "Blackie" Webb (right) confessed to murdering a woman who turned out to be alive, Jack Keen (left) was suspected of murdering a woman but was never arrested

Source - Hemet News

Beulah Foster witnessed the murder of a woman, but because she was drunk she was not considered a reliable witness

Source - Hemet News

THE

RED CIRCLE

FIEND

QUEENS, NEW YORK OCTOBER 1937

On a cool, autumn evening two teenagers parked in a well-known lovers' lane to kiss, whisper endearments, and perhaps make plans for the future that life promised them. Young and happy, this promise had yet to unfurl its petals fully for them, and there were decisions to be made, agreements to be smiled over and neither of them had reason to believe anyone could envy them their good fortune.

However someone did, perhaps someone who detested what life promised them, or worse what life had delivered so far. Someone so full of rage they shot both of the young lovers in the head, and then stabbed the girl several times in the chest. Their reward was a temporary surcease of the self-hatred and despair that ran circles in their mind like a rabid dog.

Constant fear is masked with anger and a refusal to be overlooked and ignored. So after killing Lewis Weiss, Frances Hajek and their rose-colored future, they took a lipstick and drew a circle of bright red on the forehead of each of the victims. And for good measure money was taken from each of them. Perhaps in those last moments when sanity returned, a decision was made to throw a wrench in the investigation that was sure to follow and make it look like a robbery.

On October 3, 1937, Richard Jarvis took a pleasant stroll through the woods off Grand Central Parkway and Springfield Boulevard in Queens. This area was a favorite for picnickers during the day and lovers at night, so he was surprised when he saw a car parked at a single lane auto track that lead to a clearing surrounded by maple and oak trees. It was after 1 p.m.

When he found Lewis and Frances, it confirmed the trepidation he felt from the first moment he viewed the vehicle, and the certainty he would never be able to forget what he saw. And he was right.

When police arrived, besides their first efforts which were to identify the victims, they looked for clues, especially a motive for the murder. The fact the girl had been stabbed repeatedly in the chest pointed to something darker than a simple robbery. The newspapers immediately dubbed them the Lipstick Murders because of the red circles drawn on the victims' forehead.

Police confirmed that money had been taken from Lewis' wallet, and Frances' purse had also been emptied, however jewelry had been left untouched. Robbing them perhaps had been an afterthought or a decoy, so police were wary of saying this was the motive.

William J. Burns, president of the International Detective Agency was asked for his thoughts on the crime. He told the medical examiner he believed jealousy could be a motive for the crime, and not to exclude the possibility the perpetrator was a woman. He based it on the fact that Frances was stabbed seven times with a sharp knife, possibly an ice-pick. He said, "This appears to indicate someone maddened by jealousy or congenitally insane." The very "wantoness" of the act, had elements of womanish vengeance in it. According to him, "woman slayers, as a rule, are far more vicious than men, particularly when dealing with their rivals."

His advice to law enforcement was to look closely at all the acquaintances of the victims, especially the girls.

He theorized that if it was a crime of revenge, then who the police was seeking was knowledgeable of the couple's habits, and that they planned to be near Grand Central Parkway. This would allow them to lay in wait for them, or perhaps they were trailed there from the skating ring the couple had gone to in Long Island.

Others thought that robbery was the aim of the murders. Were the circles on their forehead used to throw police off and link it to the unsolved, 3-X murders which occurred seven years ago in the same area?

Perhaps there was an admirer who Frances refused; maybe an older man, someone Frances had no interest in at all, but who became obsessed with the teenage girl. A man who knew that he could never offer her what she wanted, which was a youthful mate. Her mother said her daughter had no other suitor, and in Frances' diary which was found in her purse, the only name mentioned was Lewis.

Certain aspects of the crime pointed to premeditation. Police did not find any fingerprints on the lipstick used to mark the victims or even on the car itself. This did not speak of a younger perpetrator spurred by a desire for revenge, but someone who was careful enough to wear gloves.

When Jarvis found them, Lewis was behind the wheel, his head resting on the back of the seat. Frances' head and shoulders were on the floor of the vehicle, her feet on the ground. Her red velvet dress was disarranged and her blouse was drenched in blood from the chest wounds. The lipstick used to draw the circles lay by her feet.

Lewis Weiss was a high school honor graduate, known to be studious. He was a clerk at the American Steel and Wire Corporation, and went to school at night to study electrical engineering.

Frances was known as a sober girl who worked at her family's bakery, and attended Pratt Institute to study dress design and commercial art, three times per week.

The teenagers had been a couple for over a year. Both were the only children of their parents.

When police scoured the woods around the crime scene they found two discharged shells from a .25 caliber pistol, however the pistol itself or a knife was not located.

Police looked to their families, thinking perhaps this was an act of retribution against the parents. The Hajek family emigrated from Hungary 22 years before, and established a bakery. They lived over their business located in Queens for the last twelve years.

The Weiss were also a middle-class family from the same neighborhood. Mr. Weiss worked as a salesman.

Neither family had anything in their background or in their day-to-day dealings that would have led to the murder of their children.

Police expanded their investigation to Creedmore State Hospital, an insane asylum less than half a mile from the murder scene. Had there been a violent patient that escaped? No, all patients were accounted for, and Frances' autopsy confirmed she was not sexually assaulted. In fact she was a virgin.

A day later police questioned a retired police sergeant described as a "little touched in the head". They thought perhaps the culprit had been dressed as police officer since Weiss' wallet lay on his lap, opened to display his driver's license. Had he been ordered to produce it?

The police believed the victims had originally parked a few hundred feet off Grand Central Parkway in the Hollis woods. This was 1,000 feet from where the murders occurred. If the murderer posing as a police opened the door of the car and aimed his gun at Lewis, he could have ordered him to drive further into the woods. Once the auto traveled to an almost impassable lane to the secluded spot where the bodies were found, he then shot the boy twice in the head.

Frances would have been dragged from the car and shot twice through the right temple. Once she fell back, the culprit knifed her in the chest. Both bullets emerged from her skull; one of them was found on the seat of the car. Despite a close search, the detective could not find the other one. They couldn't find a bullet hole in the car either.

Police then looked to an organization known as the "Mystery Rollers" who were skaters in Queens Village. Police wanted to know if the symbol drawn on the victims' forehead had any connection to them. This inquiry produced no leads.

In the meantime, the Alley Pond nearby was dredged with grapples, but nothing was found.

As the police expanded their search into the woods they came upon a clearing not far from the murder scene with a recently deserted camp. A fireplace made of rough stone, held a double boiler. Nearby a pair of socks, a shirt with a laundry mark and a linen handkerchief embroidered with the initial "P" lay on a piece of tarpaulin.

On a board used as a table, police found a mound of sand. Based on its dryness they estimated the camp was abandoned within 24 hours.

Without any actual proof of who committed the murder, the identity and motive was interpreted in different ways. Lieutenant Smith who played a part in the investigation of the unsolved 3-X Murder believed the killer was young, from the neighborhood and the same age as the victims.

The more police questioned family and friends the more it became evident that both of the victims were popular and well liked.

Two days later the toxicologist's report came back which showed both of them had been drinking alcohol before their death. Frances had 2-plus alcohol in her brain, a condition which was just short of intoxication.

Lewis had considerably less, only a trace showed up in his brain. Detectives canvassed the drinking holes between Mineola and Queens Village, Long Island to see if they had stopped off there.

Later it was determined that Frances' compact which she always carried with her was missing, and police suspected the killer kept it as a trophy.

Soon the waters were muddied when self-confessed murderers stepped forward to say they were responsible for the death of the teenagers. Patrick O'Connor, 20, thought he "may have been wandering around the Hollis Woods the night of October 2, with a gun and knife". Police held him as a vagrant and sent him to Kings County Hospital for observation. After questioning him, authorities were convinced he suffered from delusions.

Within a day Betty May McCall, a carnival dancer who lived in Harlem, told police she was forced to be a spectator of the crime. She said a "35-year-old man dressed in gray, talking with a German accent" picked her up in his car at 40th Street and Second Ave. His name was Livingston and he came from 117th St. and Morningside Ave. She took police to the vicinity to find Livingston, but no trace was found of the man. Doubt was cast on her story, when she described the murder was committed with a "black handled revolver" and not an automatic pistol.

Betty McCall said that when Frances Hajek saw Livingston, she said "Oh, it's you!" before she was shot. Afterward the man "reported" to a girl named Muriel, whom he met at the Long Island City end of Queensboro Bridge. He told her, "Everything is O.K."

He gave Betty McCall the black-handled revolver and a six-inch knife which she wrapped in his handkerchief. "He gave me $25 and told me to ditch the parcel, where there wouldn't be any follow-up. I tossed them into a garbage can at 16th St. and Eighth Ave., Manhattan."

She told police, the knife belonged to her, because she carried it for self-defense, and the night of the crime he ordered her to remain in the car, took her knife and walked to another vehicle. She heard a shot from the darkness, and got out and followed him. Then she heard a girl call out a name. This story turned out to be made up.

Marjorie Whittington, former Ziegfeld show girl was later identified as a mystery woman who telephoned "eye-witness" accounts to several newspapers.

All these so called confessions and leads led to a dead end.

A few days later Harriet Wagner proprietor of the Creedmoor Restaurant near the Creedmore State Hopsital for the Insane contacted detectives and told them, "I have studied photographs of the two, and I am positive they were in my place about 11 p.m. that Saturday. They had two beers each and the boy left 40 cents to pay for their drinks."

A month after the murder police were looking at any type of violent or sexual offender.

John Simon, 15, attempted to mutilate a boy of 7 who ran off screaming. When the police came to where he told police he had been accosted they found John Simon with a 4-year-old girl in a thicket. They dragged him out before he could hurt her. The young offender fought so violently against arrest, biting both officers on the fingers, that he had to be tied hand and foot. After questioning it was found he was not involved in the Hajek-Lewis murders. The judge sent him to Bellevue for observation.

The next lead appeared on November 18, when a letter written on a cigarette wrapper was sent to Chief Inspector John J. Ryan. It was postmarked Flushing 3 p.m., November 16. It said, "Find a WPA watchman whose name starts with a 'P' and you will get information about Lipstick Case."

Detectives checked the WPA rolls and found four men whose name began with P. They along with 80 other WPA workers were near the Hollis Woods on the night of the murder were questioned, but it came to nothing.

Towards the end of December a .25 caliber automatic pistol was found in a sewer only two miles from the murder scene.

In July 1938, Walter H. Wiley, 19, was arrested in Reno, connected to an outstanding burglary warrant issued by New York. Police looked closer at him because he vanished the day the bodies of Weiss and Hajek were discovered, not reappearing until November 20, in Baltimore, where he enlisted in the army. By April 1938, he had deserted.

He told detectives he held up at least six couples in parked cars in Queens. He knew his victims would not report the crime for fear of publicity. He carried a knife and gun loaded with blanks. He denied involvement in the murder of Frances and Lewis, however later it was learned that Wiley who lived five blocks from the Hajek Bakery, often expressed admiration toward Frances.

Detectives recalled when a friend of Frances told of a "pestering suitor" who wrote her unwelcomed love poetry.

Police held Wiley without bail on a charge of looting apartments and taking $1500 worth of jewelry.

Wiley's alibi for the night of the murder collapsed. His relatives in Baltimore said he had not arrived in the city until October 20, contrary to his statement he had been there on October 2, when the murder was committed.

An unnamed Queens Village youth told police that Wiley threatened to "put a red circle on you too," when he refused to participate in a burglary.

Wiley was given a lie detector test, and based on the results the Queens District Attorney announced he would continue the investigation of Walter Wiley as a suspect in the Lipstick Murders.

Almost a year to the date of the murder Walter H. Wiley was facing charges of robbery, burglary and grand larceny. Two Good Humor ice cream vendors identified him as the man who robbed them on the night of July 21, 1937.

By March 1939, Walter Wiley had been convicted in the hold up of the ice cream vendors. He denied committing the murders, and there was not enough evidence to press charges against him for the crime.

Eventually he was sentenced to a total of 25 to 40 years in Sing Sing prison on charges of robbery, burglary and grand larceny.

Walter was serving time in Sing Sing Prison in 1940, however three years after this he was living in Florida, where he married and died three decades later.

The murder of Frances Hajek and Lewis Weiss
baffled police due to its lack of motive.
Source - The Record

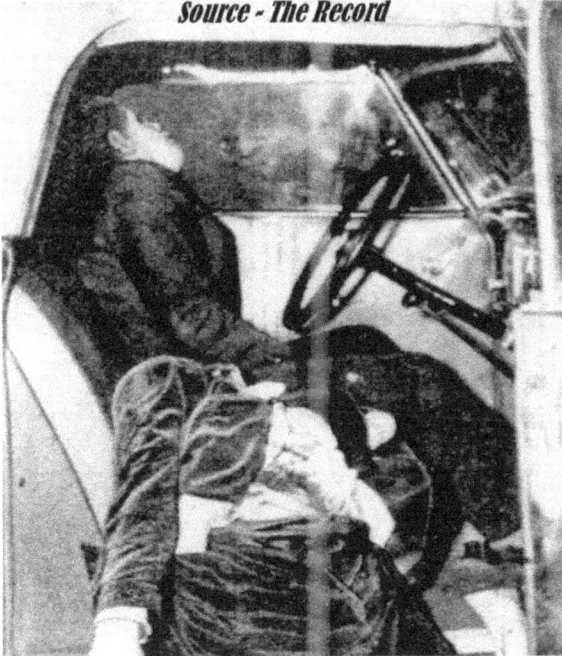

Walter H. Wiley, 19, lied about several of his alibis.
The murderer used Frances' lipstick to mark his victims
Source - The Record

DEATH ON THE PISTOL RANGE

TAMPA, FLORIDA MARCH 1929

Edward G. Steward, 47, president of the Steward Mellon Marble & Tile Company traveled on rain slicked Platt Street in Tampa. Suddenly there was a screech of tires, and Steward's body was flung from his vehicle and landed headfirst on the pavement. A car belonging to W. B. Swem, a snowbird from New Jersey, struck Steward's car as it crossed Hyde Park Avenue.

Swem was unhurt; however Steward was dead as a result of a major fracture of the skull. He left behind four children. His widow Hattie, was bequeathed with his entire estate. Within two weeks of her husband's demise, Mrs. Steward had filed a lawsuit against Swem for $75,000, even though an initial investigation found the accident was unavoidable.

Hattie Steward continued on with her life. She was a member of Tampa's Ladies' Social Bunco Club, and after her husband's death the only mention of her name in the newspapers was coupled with social activities.

That was accurate until January 1, 1931.

A little after 10 p.m. on New Year's Day, city detective John E. Jones, 52, sat in a car parked on the outskirts of Tampa. The spot was the old police pistol range, a cleared field miles from the nearest house. Next to him was a robust woman wearing an orange dress, dark brown coat trimmed in fur and a brown felt hat. Her name was Hattie Steward.

Perhaps they met in that lonely spot since Detective Jones was a married man. Whatever the reason, they were well preoccupied because a stranger snuck up on them and shot a pistol close to a dozen times through the closed window. Jones was struck several times and died instantly.

What Mrs. Steward later told police was, "It appeared to be a woman dressed in men's clothing, who spoke in a high-pitched voice."

She described how she took Jones' revolver which was lying on the seat beside him and fired five times to attract attention, but unable to summon help she ran to the road to try to stop a passing car. Finally a motorist took her to the nearby Four Brothers Cafe where she called police.

Mrs. Steward was taken to the county jail and then transported to the Tampa hospital for an x-ray, where it appeared a bullet grazed her above the hip. A county physician dressed her wound and she returned with the police to the scene of the crime.

She ran to Jones' body, which had been removed from the car and laid on the ground by fellow officers. She knelt next to it, and sobbed, "Poor old daddy, they never gave you a chance. Oh, if you could only speak and tell them who did it."

Hattie Steward repeated the story to the police. "We had been sitting here for about 20 minutes talking. He was under the wheel and I was sitting beside him. His overcoat and hat were in the back seat. He had not worn the coat all evening. He asked me turn on the dome light of the car to see what time it was, before I could turn it on, suddenly a small face pushed up close to the glass on the door. I saw it. He wore a cap and it was pulled down over his face."

"In a squeaky voice that sounded like a woman, as if he was trying to disguise it, the man hollered out, 'Now I've got you where I want you.' Then he started shooting fast. I don't know how many shots were fired. There must have been a half dozen anyway. I didn't see the man disappear. I guess I was too excited. I asked Jones if he was hurt. He didn't answer. His gun was lying on the seat between us. I picked it up and fired all the bullets in it. I was trying to attract attention."

She had given him the pistol as a birthday present.

"Nobody heard me so I ran over to Michigan Avenue and tried to flag down some cars. They wouldn't stop so I started running and then walking to town." She described she got lost before someone gave her a ride.

Hattie Steward said she knew Detective Jones four years. They ate a New Year's dinner at her home, and went for a ride, stopping at roadhouse near Horseshoe Lake. While there Jones bought a pint of liquor, however the owner of the place denied that either of them had been there at all. They ended up at the pistol range where they regularly parked.

Sheriff Joughin found glass from the broken car window, outside instead of inside the auto and on the seat. When he asked Hattie Steward about this, she had no explanation about it.

Five exploded cartridges of .32 caliber were found beside the car. Jones' gun was a .38 police special Smith & Wesson revolver.

Jones had been separated from his wife for several months. He left behind four children. He came to Tampa from Birmingham where he served as a city detective for ten years. He was well-like in the police department, and not known to have any enemies.

After examination of Jones' body, it was found that seven bullets had entered his body. The wounds in his back were in perfect alignment about three inches apart.

Later it turned out that Hattie Steward had a bullet lodged above her right hip.

Authorities were convinced the shooter was sitting in the rear seat of the car and held the pistol close to Jones' back. The left front window had a bullet hole in it near the bottom. Pieces of glass were lying on the running board and in the grass, which contradicted Hattie Steward's story the perpetrator had stood outside the car. Jones' suit also had powder burns indicating the shooter was very close to him.

Mrs. Steward said she saw no one around the car before or after the shooting, despite a new moon lighted up the area. In the twenty minutes they were parked, she noticed one car drove west on Michigan Avenue and disappeared.

The detectives who worked with Jones described him as a very cautious man. He always kept his pistol close by, and he had several years of experience in law enforcement. There was speculation if his murder was tied to his relationship with Mrs. Steward, or if it was related to any case he was working on. They also checked phone calls that came into the police station the day before.

There was one caller who declined to leave a number but asked that Jones be notified that "Charlie is waiting for him at the house." When given the message, Jones tore it up and tossed it into a trash can. He remarked, "I know a hundred Charlies, why didn't he leave a number?"

By January 4, Hattie Steward, who was held in the county jail in connection to the murder, had lawyered up and refused to make any further comments. The next day Detective Jones was buried, and by January 8, Mrs. Steward was released and the charge of first degree murder was dropped. It was also determined the wound in her back lacked powder burns. Apparently the bullet had passed through Jones' shoulder and came out his right side and then lodged itself in her hip area.

With her release the police had no other leads to follow. They offered $500 for information leading to an arrest, but none came forward.

The newspapers were describing the culprit as one of the cleverest criminals, who assassinated a police detective on a clear, moonlight night, wounded another person and escaped from an open field and with no other clues left behind beside the five cartridges found in the auto.

The police maintained the killer had to be inside the car, and not outside as Hattie Steward described. They believed the slayer rode several miles concealed behind them.

Authorities then turned their attention to Jones' wife, Minnie. They picked her up after her husband's funeral, which she attended with their son Bob Jones who was serving time in the federal penitentiary on liquor charges, and was brought by marshals to attend his father's funeral.

Eventually they released her. The couple had been separated for two years, but Mrs. Jones said the possibility of reconciliation had grown during the last few weeks. She had filed suit for separate maintenance in May 1930, but a final decree had not been entered in circuit court. Mrs. Steward was named as the cause for their estrangement. The complaint stated that Jones had formed an attachment to Hattie Steward after they were introduced by Minnie Jones herself. There was an incident where Mrs. Steward came to visit Jones at home where he was recuperating from an illness, and Minnie Jones caught them kissing. They admitted to her their mutual attraction.

Without clues, the police were left only with questions surrounding the murder of Detective Jones. Was he killed because of his attentions to Hattie Steward? Was he killed due to troubles in his own family? Did a criminal kill him because of his police work, or did he just pick the wrong place to use as a rendezvous point?

The case remained stagnant for a year until January 1932 when "Hard Sam" Daugherty, 52, was arrested in Miami. He was a former Tampa bootlegger and son of an Atlanta saloon keeper. Authorities were searching for him throughout the country for two months, related to the murder of Detective Jones.

Daugherty had been charged various times in federal court on liquor cases, and once was arrested after a fist fight with prohibition officers. While on a suspended 12-month sentence, he was accused with four others which included Jones' son, Robert "Bob" Jones in the kidnapping in August 1930, of George Kite, a prohibition informer.

Robert Jones was sentenced to five years. Daugherty was acquitted after proving he had been to a picture show the night of the kidnapping. The rumor was that he had turned state's evidence against the other men.

Daugherty denied any connection to the murder. He said, "I didn't do this. I had no idea I was suspected and didn't know it until I got back here this morning. Why 'Skinny' Jones and I were friends. We kidded each other a lot. I never had any thought of killing him. I couldn't have a reason for doing it."

The state attorney and other officials made little headway in obtaining evidence to link Daugherty with Jones' murder. They were able to hold him on a warrant issued by the US Marshal's office on liquor charges. At the end of January the charges were dropped.

Daugherty's good luck persisted when a federal judge disposed of the liquor charges against him by suspending his one year sentence and directing him to report on a monthly basis to a prohibition agent. But that luck ended suddenly in July, 1932 when he engaged in a gun and knife fight with his estranged wife Irene. He was shot in the shoulder, and when he arrived at the Tampa hospital he claimed the wound was self inflicted, however his wife was arrested.

She claimed she shot him in self-defense against a knife attack. He entered the home he no longer lived at around 2 in the morning, and she saw him in a mirror. She chased him with a gun, firing off several shots, one which hit him.

Outside police found his car with his shoes next to it. He told them, "I didn't want to die with my boots on," but police believed he did it in order to sneak inside his wife's room.

She lived upstairs from a palatial speakeasy on Azeele Street that she decorated in a lavish fashion.

The knife Daugherty brought with him was a long blade, and his wife showed police scars where he had wounded her in previous attacks.

Life was not dull for Hard Sam Daugherty. During those days he'd been attacked twice by other Tampa gangsters. Once in the downtown area and another occasion at a lonely spot on Memorial Highway.

Soon after Irene Daugherty filed divorce proceedings against him citing cruelty. The case showed they were married in Cleveland on August 6, 1926 when she was fourteen years old and he was forty-nine. The complaint stated, "During the last three or four years he has abused her by scolding, intimidating and inflicting bodily violence on her on numerous occasions." The previous January she charged, "The defendant did strike her with his fist, inflicting severe pain and bruises on her body, cursing and appearing at her home and did there shoot out the lights, tear down the light fixtures and shoot out the windows."

Six months later Daugherty was involved in a shoot out with another gangster, Howard Rice, 28 on Florida Avenue between Zack and Polk Street. He was struck in the right hand and in both legs by three bullets. At the hospital he told police his wife Irene and Rice were sitting in a parked car on Florida Avenue when he passed by and Rice opened fire. He ended up sentenced to a year for violating his federal parole.

Daugherty had a hard time staying out of trouble. In the following years he was charged with voting twice (he couldn't vote at all since he was a felon), and fleeing from a hit and run while under the influence of liquor. Unfortunately he hit a vehicle being driven by Judge Watkins.

Like a one-man wrecking ball, trouble followed in his footsteps. In February 1935, he ran the Black Cat Cafe on Lafayette and Pierce Streets in Tampa. He was shot by a man in his shoulder as he ascended the stairs to his living quarters.

It seemed that Hard Sam Daugherty was guilty of many things, but not killing Detective Jones. The years slipped by and the case remained unsolved.

Then a confession in 1947 revived Tampa's most mysterious slaying until that date. By then the state attorney and the city detective in charge of the Jones' case had passed away.

A prisoner serving a long sentence in Alcatraz admitted to the murder. His name was Ramon "Raymond" Remine.

FBI agents probing the 1931 case were surprised when they found all records had disappeared. Tampa officials said that in those years, notes were scanty at best and there were very few records of fingerprints kept. However the files were also missing in the office of the State Attorney.

Despite the investigation by the FBI, the detectives were unconvinced of the sincerity of Remine's confession. He was set to serve a stint at the Rock until 1964.

In his confession Remine described where he shot Detective Jones after a botched robbery attempt, and his story dovetailed very neatly with the known facts of the case. Unfortunately the 1931 case records which had mysteriously disappeared also included the name of several persons who were picked up and later released. Was Ramon Remine one of them?

In June 1948, State Attorney Farrior, during an election campaign speech said the murder of Detective John E. Jones was a closed case. It seemed that since making the confession Remine was diagnosed as a "psychotic case" and not deemed a reliable source.

According to the prison guards in Alcatraz, Remine lived in constant fear he would die at the hands of one of the inmates, because they believed he told FBI details of a conspiracy that led to a large-scale riot at the prison. Remine was assigned, at his own insistence, to the isolation and hospital wards. After the last time he was denied to be kept in isolation, he made the admission concerning the Jones case.

However Remine told officials in considerable detail how the shooting took place. During the confession Remine told his chaplain he wanted to be electrocuted for his Florida crime. Part of his retelling of the shooting contained an element of self-defense. He described that with another man named Ward, they went to the car to "have some fun" by scaring the occupants who were in a compromising position.

In those days he traveled through Tampa as a representative of a novelty company refilling vending machines. He said that Jones opened fire on them, and that in turn they emptied their guns at the detective as they fled. He was vague about other details. In actuality Jones never fired his gun.

Officials did establish from Walter Gulick, Remine's boss that he had been in Tampa when the crime was committed. He was accompanied by a woman, who he believed was his wife. He was going by the name of John Traynor.

Gulick complained that Remine got into a lot of trouble when he opened fire on a detective in Des Moines, shortly after the murder of Detective Jones.

Mr. Gulick did leave out a little detail, which was that in 1931 he pulled a bank heist with Remine of the Ely Savings Bank in Iowa. Remine was using several aliases such as John Traynor, Jack Hines and Jack Reline. Remine had engaged in a gun battle with police.

Authorities eventually found the woman who accompanied Remine while he was in Florida. Her name was Minnie Stevens Traynor. She said that after the days of the detective's murder, Remine's behavior was suspicious and he refused to let her see newspapers when they left the state and traveled north. Since then she'd become a respectable housewife and lived in a small Midwest town.

Like Gulick, she omitted to tell police of her activities while in league with Ramon Remine. In March 1932, when she was 20 years old, she was convicted on a charge of kidnapping in connection with the abduction of Lyle Proud, a taxicab driver. She helped her husband John Traynor to escape from the Olmsted county jail where they forced the taxi driver at the point of a gun to drive them 100 miles away.

Traynor (Remine) was sentenced to serve a 30-year term in Fort Madison, Iowa on his plea of guilty to shooting a Des Moines detective.

The State Attorney without explaining why they were closing the Jones case determined that the probability of getting a death sentence 17 years after the crime took place was small. The former Mrs. Traynor (Remine) could not be compelled to testify, and her present spouse did not want her involved in the case.

Somewhere in the midst of this investigation, Hattie Steward probably told them she couldn't or wouldn't testify about a crime that took place almost two decades before.

Despite the warden's warning that Remine, though psychotic was dangerous, he was given parole. In June 1955, he single-handedly robbed the Mount Auburn, Iowa Savings Bank of almost $12,000. He also violated his parole for the bank robberies committed in Tennessee. The law caught up with him in September of that year. The sixty-one year old was described by the FBI as "one of the most wanted bank robbers in the nation."

The FBI were given a tip of his whereabouts by an optometrist with whom Remine had made an appointment to change his eyes from brown to green with the use of contact lenses.

He returned to jail, and due to failing health he was eventually transferred to the medical center for federal prisoners in Springfield, Missouri. He died in 1964.

The murder of Detective Jones remains unsolved. The only witness to the crime was Hattie Steward and she died in 1960, taking her secrets to the grave.

Detective Jones was shot and killed at close range while in the company of wealthy widow Hattie Steward while they were parked on a deserted police range
Source - Evening Independent

Tampa in the 1930s (above) Mrs. Minnie Jones (left) was considered only for a short time a suspect in the shooting of her husband.

Source - Evening Independent

117

"HARD SAM" DAUGHERTY

Hard "Sam" Daugherty and Ramon Remine were considered suspects in the shooting of Detective Jones

Source - Evening Independent

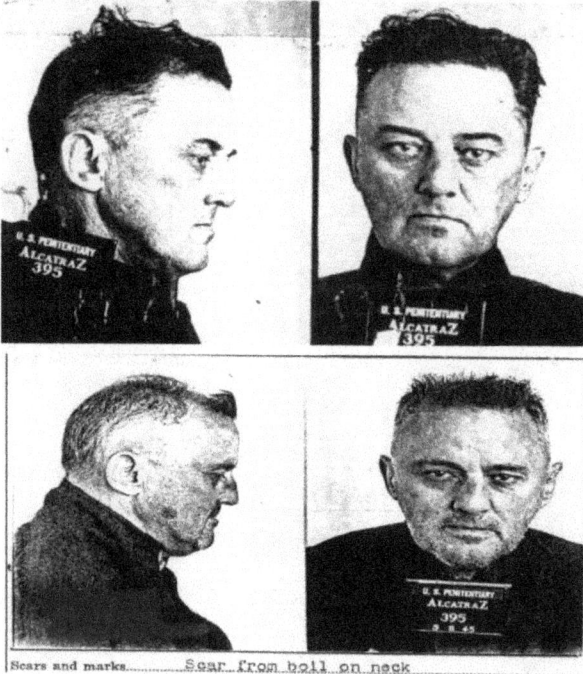

Scars and marks........ Scar from boil on neck

BOOTLEGGERS' CANYON

LOS ANGELES CALIFORNIA NOVEMBER 29, 1929

On Thanksgiving Day hikers traversing Pacoima Canyon stopped to eat. Close by they observed buzzards flying in a lazy circle over what they assumed to be perhaps the carcass of an animal. They walked over to see what it was, and instead discovered a headless body.

Within a few hours, the small canyon four miles northeast of San Fernando near the Pacoima Dam was overrun with police. Identification of the corpse was possible because automobile papers were found in the pocket of a sweater draped over it. His name was Carlos "Charlie" Alvarez, and he was an 18 years old musician.

The next day the police scoured the same spot, commonly known as Bootleggers' Canyon hoping to find the boy's head. Instead they found two shallow graves. A leg bone poked through the dirt piled on top of one of them. Another hole had been dug beside it. Nearby a broken shovel was found.

Enough of the bone lay exposed to indicate it was a woman. With the identity of the first victim, the police accurately surmised the woman buried in the arroyo to be his mother, Helena Alvarez-Garcia. The other shallow grave most probably contained his younger sisters, Carmelita, 12, and Alisa, 6. During the weeks the bodies lay in their hidden graves, coyotes and other animals dug up the remains and tore them apart, strewing bones along the brush.

The mystery surrounding this family started in October when Mrs. Garcia and her children disappeared from their home at 1434 Griffith Street, San Fernando. Mr. Garcia notified the police that his wife left with her children in a car his step-son had bought the month before.

Police searched the area around the home, and a place nearby described as "a wasteland where countless bootleggers were reported to operate their stills in virtual safety from police, sheriffs and federal agents". They found the abandoned car, and it was returned to the auto dealer. He told them that when he came to the home to collect on the overdue car payment, Luciano Garcia told him Carlos, his stepson had convinced his wife to leave with him and take the girls. The police searched for the family, but no clue was found to indicate their whereabouts.

Now with the discovery of the bodies almost two months later it was evident they had not run away. The police returned to speak to Mr. Garcia, their prime suspect, but he could not be found. His acquaintances said he was last seen about October 15.

Police then questioned Manuel Flores who worked at the same ranch as Luciano Garcia, and who once boarded with the family. Flores told them the couple quarreled bitterly over Mr. Garcia's attitude towards the children, especially the eldest girl Carmelita. Luciano was stepfather to the older children, and only Alisa was his daughter. Flores said Garcia told him he was going to work on a ranch near Azusa, and that was the last he saw of him.

Marion Vasquez, Charlie's girlfriend, corroborated the story of the frequent arguments between Helena and her husband, who was described as always being in a bad mood.

The police mounted a state-wide search for Luciano Garcia, which came to an unexpected end only a few days later when his body was found in a shallow grave in Rabbit Acres, a mile south of Azusa with two bullets in his head. Now it appeared that Garcia instead of being the perpetrator was a victim as well.

The authorities now searched for an "insane murderer" who executed the wholesale killing of the five members of the Garcia-Alvarez family.

Like the other bodies, there was advance decomposition of the remains, so the only clue police had to use for identification were papers found in his pocket. The police waited for further confirmation that indeed this was Luciano Garcia, since they were wary if perhaps this was a decoy left by Garcia to fake his own death.

If it was him, police did not discount the possibility that robbery was a motive, since Luciano Garcia was found to have $10 in his pocket; however his co-worker Flores said he carried $150 with him when he went to Azusa to seek work on a ranch.

During their investigation deputies spoke to a neighbor of the family who told of seeing the family leave in a truck with a mysterious man. The description of the man matched one seen around the Guichapa home. Dolores "Lola" Guichapa (Guichata) identified him as Armando Boltares. With this information they tracked him down.

He was arrested only minutes from departing on a trip that would take him 180 miles eastward to a secluded mining camp. He left a pool hall, and was sitting on a curbstone in front of the old Pico House waiting for his ride.

On December 5, Armando Boltares, a 24-year-old truck driver confessed he beat Helena Alvarez-Garcia with a club, as well as her three children, Carlos, Carmelita and Alisa. He decapitated their bodies and buried them in the shallow ditches where they were found in Pacoima Canyon. He then traced Luciano Garcia to Azusa, shot him, and buried the body on the ranch where he was employed at.

Boltares said his actions were a result of an old grudge. He said two years before, he boarded at the Garcia home and Helena induced him to withdraw $1000 from his bank account. He believed they wanted to rob him, and in the end were putting a slow poison in his food in order to get the money. Helena also tried to come between him and his girlfriend Dolores Guichapa. He went on to tell police that he planned his vengeance for months, waiting until he moved from their home.

Unsure if Dolores Guichapa was involved in the crime, both of them were booked on suspicion of murder, especially after it was determined she cooperated with police only after Boltares told her he was leaving. Did she have a hand in the murders?

In his confession he described how on October 9, he told Mrs. Garcia he could dig up a gallon of wine in Bootleggers' Canyon. He convinced her to bring the children along. Charlie followed in his car.

They arrived in the hidden arroyo around twilight, and he indicated to Charlie where he should dig. He told police, "When he stooped over to dig for the wine, I hit him with a shovel I carried, and he rolled over dead. Then I went back down the canyon and told Mrs. Garcia, Charley needed help. When she came up near him I hit her with the shovel too and she fell. Carmelita began screaming and fighting me, so I had to hit her. Then the little one began whimpering and I killed her."

He hastily buried the bodies, took some things from Carlos' car and drove to Dolores Guichapa's home where he was living.

Boltares anticipated that Luciano Garcia would search for his family, and that eventually he would go to Azusa. On October 14, his patience was rewarded and he convinced Garcia he could help him find his family. He volunteered his truck to take him to Rabbit Acres.

He told police, "When we got there, I asked him if he had a gun. He replied 'No'. So I said, 'well, that's too bad. I am going to kill you.' Then quickly I shot him in the head and buried him".

The killer described how he took the dead man's hat and scrubbed off bloody gout etched on the truck fender. He drove back to his girlfriend's house, and told her everything he did. Afterward he took her to view the grave.

Police now believed that Boltares knew something about an incident where four sticks of dynamite were placed in a priest's automobile in January; however nothing else came of this inquiry with the murder of five people hanging over his head.

Captain Bright of the sheriff's homicide division filed formal charges against Armando Boltares, 24, and his sweetheart, Dolores Guichapa, 35, for the murder of the five family members.

Soon after his initial confession, Boltares accused his girlfriend of assisting in the massacre of the mother and the children, and urging him to kill Garcia before he discovered what happened to his family. He gave the motive of Guichapa's enmity toward the family as stemming from a report Helena Garcia made against Dolores for bootlegging. He said she was the master plotter and they schemed how to commit the murder for over a year.

Every day that passed Boltares would amplify his accusation. He said Guichapa had been in charge of the plot to kill the family, all because they informed on her and she ended up getting arrested. She instructed him to dig three graves in Bootleggers' Canyon, and that she would help him lure Helena and her children to the spot where they would be killed.

He said that after murdering Charlie and his mother, he was unsure what to do with the two girls, and that Guichapa told him, "Kill them". He protested, saying, "It was a little too much to kill so many". But Guichapa insisted he finish the job. Carmelita overheard their conversation and started screaming. He told Captain Bright, "I had to kill her, and when she fell dying her small sister ran and bent over the body crying. So I hit her with the shovel too."

They buried the mother and the two girls, but night fell and they left Charlie's body lying in the brush.

At the inquest, Boltares repeated his confession to the crime, including Dolores Guichapa's part in it. She kept denying her involvement in what was called a "venganza" or Mexican family feud. All she kept saying about Boltares is that he was crazy.

Charging the pair was suspended until it could be clarified what part each had played in the crime, in order to charge them accordingly. In the meantime, Dolores was sued for divorce by her husband Refugio Zarate.

The judge ordered Boltares to undergo a psychiatric examination, following his plea of insanity. A week later two alienists delivered an initial report describing Boltares as sub-normal mentally.

In mid-February, during the sanity hearing, Dr. Victor Parkin, expert witness for the defense, testified the accused had not responded normally to reflex tests, but that that he did know the difference between right and wrong.

Another defense witness was Jesus Navarra, an acquaintance of Boltares, he testified he made a chance remark about the slayings, and that Boltares took it as an accusation. He drew his gun and fired three shots, and that lucky for him went wild.

Another doctor testified that Boltares during his incarceration was hallucinating that his hair had fallen out and he was bald.

The prosecution called A. G. Rivera, court interpreter, who testified that Boltares appeared to be normal and answered all the questions quickly and clearly during the proceedings.

He was declared sane, and the prosecution decided to dismiss the charges against Dolores Guichapa, as there was no evidence produced to support Boltares' accusations against her.

Boltares was found guilty of five charges of murder and sentenced to death. He was sent to San Quentin, and he died on the gallows on May 16, 1930. He wrote three letters the night before the execution, one to his mother in Los Angeles, one to his wife and one to an unnamed friend in Mexico. Their contents were not disclosed.

In the courtroom after he was sentenced to die, Boltares disclosed to a burning love for Dolores Guichapa. His infatuation with her, led to the revenge killing of the family because Helena Garcia had reported about his girlfriend's bootlegging activity that resulted in her arrest. He finally disclosed what happened on the day of the murder.

He invited Dolores, Helena and the three children to accompany him on a ride to Bootleggers' Canyon. While the women talked, he led Alisa, Carlos and Carmelita out of sight around a bend, and crushed their skulls with a spade and slit their throats with a razor. He returned and killed Helena with the same weapon. He then drove Dolores back home.

HE ADMITS KILLING
FAMILY FOR GRUDGE

Armando Boltares

Armando Boltares killed siblings Carlos, Carmelita and Alisa because of a grudge. C.1929

Source - Lincoln County Leader

Armando
Boltares
Mug
Shot
c.1930

48176

Bolares was arrested sitting at the curb outside the Pico House. He was about to leave for a mining town 160 miles away

SIX DIFFERENT WAYS TO KILL YOUR WIFE

SAN BERNARDINO, CA. JANUARY 1946

It was New Year's Day and Williamson and Marshall Braun were enroute to Big Bear. They stopped at a clearing on High Gear Road, a half mile from Arrowhead Springs Hotel, just off Rim of the World Highway.

Williamson heard a creek flowing down the canyon and stepped over to see it. He called out to his companion, "My God, I've found the body of a woman." She lay wrapped in a green, plaid blanket, which was tied around her hips and stomach. Her head and hands were missing. His companion urged him not to go down in case they would erase clues.

They alerted Leo Flattery of the forest service, who in turn called the police.

At the top of the bank, officers found a 10-foot piece of twine stained with blood. The roll down the embankment covered the corpse with dirt and twigs. A scrub oak stopped its descent 20 feet from the bottom.

129

The body was taken to Kremer's Mortuary where the county autopsy surgeon believed the head and hands were hacked off with either a cleaver, or another heavy instrument. The intent was obviously to prevent identifying her.

She was described as weighing 130 to 145 pounds, with a medium build, and large bunions on both feet. She stood at 5'6" to 5'8". Apart from the wounds she had a small lesion on her left shin, a vaccination scar and two bruises on her knee. They believed she had brown hair.

A .38 blue steel jacket slug entered her left armpit and became lodged in her chest. The other which caused death, entered her left breast, piercing her heart, liver and spine. She had powder burns on her skin indicating she'd been shot at close range.

Rigor mortis had not set in leading the police to believe she'd been thrown down the ravine during the night.

While the police tried to find other clues, especially the missing head and hands, they checked reports on missing women. Tips came in, but were dismissed because they didn't fit the description of the victim.

A second autopsy was performed and it was found her neck was cut at the junction of the fifth and sixth cervical vertebrae, and then downward through the larynx.

3 WEEKS LATER

Arthur L. Eggers, a clerk in the Temple City Sheriff's Office lived at 202 North Rosemead Blvd., Temple City. He reported his wife Dorothy Eggers, 42, missing on December 30. They had been married for 18 years, and adopted two children, Marie, 18, and Lorraine, 11.

His co-workers looked closer at the missing person's report he submitted, and thought it strange he listed her height as 5'2" when they knew she was taller, measuring at least 5'7".

Two days later the headless body was found and fellow deputies and clerks at the Temple City Sheriff's substation became suspicious, especially when they noticed discrepancies in his replies to their casual questions about his wife. They recalled he once said he worked as a butcher. Strangely though, Mr. Eggers was considered a mild-mannered man who'd been employed by the police department for ten years.

He told them he went to view the headless corpse at the San Bernardino's sheriff's office and said, "It wasn't Dorothy." Later they learned the body was held at a private mortuary, not in the police department's basement as he claimed.

The sheriffs at Temple Station in an "unofficial" investigation located Dr. Clarence Carmichael who treated Mrs. Eggers, and took him to San Bernardino to view the corpse. He recognized a scar on her lower right shin.

They came to Sheriff Biscailuz, their supervisor with their concerns and he in turn contacted the San Bernardino police.

They brought Eggers in for questioning, and when asked if he'd done away with his wife, Eggers responded, "I wouldn't hurt a hair on her head. I wouldn't kill her. I wanted her there to raise the children."

Both daughters confirmed the blanket tied around the body came from their home. They made the statement in Eggers' presence who accused them of lying. The girls told police they last saw their mother late on the night of December 29.

After this interview they took him to the police department in San Bernardino.

Once there the questioning continued, and he admitted he once owned a .38 automatic pistol that he had since sold.

Other damning evidence surfaced to point the finger at Arthur Eggers as a murderer. Stains found inside their home proved to be human blood. It matched blotches inside the family car, which he sold after his wife disappeared. The cover was missing from the auto's rear seat.

He described where he quarreled with Dorothy on December 29, when he returned from work around 1 a.m. Upset about the fight he took the car and "drove all night, going as far as Long Beach". When he returned home at 9 a.m. his wife was gone.

Dorothy Eggers' family last saw them on Christmas Day when they held a party at their home. Everyone described them as being in "fine spirits". When asked about Arthur Eggers, like his co-workers they said, "He's a mild sort of fellow", who when his wife became angry, simply "passed it off".

"Dorothy's the one who had a temper," her family said.

Her 70-year-old mother tearfully described, after refusing to view the body, "I can't believe it. They had their quarrels, but I don't think Arthur would do a thing like that."

Despite the disbelief of Dorothy's family that he could have murdered her, other facts surfaced. He forged her signature to transfer ownership of the auto. The workers at the Pasadena office of the Department of Motor Vehicles said he was accompanied by a young woman matching the description of his eldest daughter. But they told police he called her several times by the name of "Dorothy."

Police planned to open water drains at the Eggers house to search for human blood and tissue. They dug in the back yard in search of Mrs. Eggers' head and hands.

Another witness identified the body. Lester Loomis, 42, who roomed at the Eggers' home for two years confirmed it was Dorothy.

The police finally took Arthur Eggers to view the body and he studied it dispassionately for a few minutes. Then he told the sheriff he would identify it as his wife's body if he was not suspected to be the killer. From there police took him to the top of the canyon off the Rim of the World Highway. In a calm voice he commented, "What a heck of a place to dump a body. There are a lot better spots."

Despite the mounting evidence against Arthur Eggers, Captain Bowers told reporters Dorothy Eggers' name had been linked romantically with another man just before her disappearance.

The accused man defended himself by insisting his wife may have been murdered by a soldier she previously entertained at their house when he was at work. Or perhaps she met her end when she refused the advances of the wrong man "while on one of her numerous hitch-hiking trips".

He told authorities the soldier had served in India, and then went overseas, but corresponded with his wife while he was away, and visited her upon his return.

Police had the man's name and serial number, and they followed up on the lead, in order to make sure the right person was charged with the crime.

The adopted daughters confirmed the man had visited the house twice in December, and that "he was quite a good looking guy."

Booked as a suspect on January 25, Eggers agreed to take a lie detector test, but after being grilled for five hours at the old Central Jail, the efforts failed to crack his story. The prosecutor changed the charge from murder to grand theft based on the sale of the automobile belonging to his wife where her signature was forged.

Two days later everything changed. Captain Gordon Bowers of the sheriff's homicide detail announced to the press that Arthur Eggers confessed to slaying his wife. He agreed to take police to a distant canyon where he buried his wife's head and hands. However after searching for hours in the area he indicated, they came up with nothing. Another trip was taken to Fish Canyon to locate the gun he used to kill her.

Eggers than changed his story and said he burned them in an incinerator at his home. He kept the fire burning for three days, then scattered the ashes in the yard of his home. The remaining bone fragments were buried.

The justification Eggers gave for killing the woman he'd been married to for close to twenty years, started when he saw a man slip out of his home a little after midnight on December 30.

An anger he never felt before engulfed him and he slapped and beat her. She fought back and taunted him by saying he was a "cheap skate", and that she would continue in any affair with any man she chose. He knocked her down, and she fled into the bathroom. He grabbed his pistol and followed her.

"I was never so mad, crazy mad," he said. "I shot her. When she fell into the bathtub, I shot her again." Killing her did not calm his anger, and he decided to "cut her to pieces and scatter the pieces along the highways, anywhere." When he stuffed the corpse into the luggage compartment of the automobile, her head stuck out. He used a carpenter's saw and severed the head, neck and shoulders. He then sawed off the hands.

Five days later the pistol and saw he used were found in Little Santa Anita Canyon, north of Arcadia. They were wrapped in newspaper.

It came out that Dorothy Eggers called her husband an "insect", failing to see there was a fearsome monster simmering underneath his undisclosed anger. After sending the police on a wild goose chase for the missing body parts, he clammed up and refused to tell the police where he disposed of them.

The police suspected that perhaps Arthur Eggers tortured his wife before killing her, and this was the real reason he refused to give more information to the police.

The evidence kept mounting. A wrist watch belonging to Dorothy was found in her husband's locker at work, and her rings at a pawn shop.

On February 2, he was indicted for murder by the grand jury.

Then Eggers threw a wrench into the wheels of justice when a few days later he switched attorneys. John Rotchford, his long time friend, had represented him and was the one who urged him to confess. He then hired James Starritt and this tactic got him a continuance.

On February 13, Eggers moved to have the charge of murder dismissed. The submissive man, who gave six different versions of killing and dismembering his wife, declared he planned to fight his indictment. He refused to enter a plea, and after glancing defiantly around the court room, he stomped into the prisoners' pen.

James Starritt argued the grand jury received secondary and hearsay evidence. "That body might be the headless horseman of Sleepy Hollow, for all this transcript shows. This record does not even show she was missing."

The judge denied the motion to quash the indictment, but found fault with the method in which the confession was obtained.

The indignities visited on Dorothy Eggers did not end with her murder. On March 8, her mutilated, but embalmed body was returned to the coroner by an undertaker who said he had not been paid for its burial. The undertaker in turn sent it to the county morgue where it was stored.

March 20, at his arraignment Eggers pled not guilty by reason of insanity. The judge appointed three alienists to examine his mental condition.

A day later, Arthur's sister Grace Gaggetti died of a heart attack. Five minutes later, her husband George dropped dead. Another Eggers brother, Frederick had already passed away in October 1944.

May 7, the case went to trial and the state asked for the death penalty.

In his opening statement to the jury made up of 10 women and 2 men, the defense attorney told the jury, "Our evidence will prove Mrs. Eggers was a domineering, forceful woman who was not adverse to attending dances alone and picking up strange men. For a long time Eggers heard rumors of his wife's unfaithfulness. When he saw with his own eyes the truth of these rumors there was a blinding flash in his mind and he grabbed a gun to defend the sanctity of his home. In the struggle Mrs. Eggers, who was strong physically, was accidentally shot".

The children were not spared. Eleven-year-old Lorraine testified in court the blanket in which the body was found came from her bed. The other daughter demonstrated to the jury how her foster father made her practice writing Dorothy's signature. Eventually he signed the title to the vehicle himself.

Ray Pinker, a police chemist testified he found fragments of human bones imbedded in the .38 caliber revolver recovered and identified as the death weapon. He also found traces of blood and skin tissue. The prosecutor contended Eggers beat his wife with the gun after shooting her.

In a surprise twist when Arthur Eggers took the stand he said the torso discovered at the ravine was not his wife's. This came after his attorney admitted Eggers killed his wife in a struggle for the weapon.

At the conclusion of the case, the deputy district attorney read an alleged statement by Eggers that said, "either the murder of my wife was premeditated or it was done by a maniac or sadist, and I am no maniac."

On May 30, Arthur Eggers was found guilty of murdering his wife. The jury deliberated for two days. His defense asked the jury to decide he was insane and thus allow him to avoid death in California's gas chamber.

The doctors who examined him found he was mentally unbalanced when he committed the crime. Without a recommendation from the jury for leniency it automatically carried a death penalty.

With the possibility of execution hanging over his head Eggers tendered his resignation to Sheriff Biscailuz, to become effective immediately. He requested that back pay, vacation and retirement fund should be mailed to him at the county jail.

Etta Eggers, Arthur's sister testified at the sanity trial, that her brother had sustained several head injuries in childhood, and one of them left him unconscious for several hours. She said their father Frederick, former San Francisco county sheriff, "acted in an erratic manner" as well. It was evident she was trying to provide a genetic predisposition as to why her brother had committed this horrible crime.

The three psychiatrists assigned to examine Arthur concluded he was sane, and on June 30, the court upheld their verdict which would result in a death sentence.

However Eggers was still fighting the inevitable. He charged a woman juror was ineligible. The defense filed a motion for a new trial along with an affidavit signed by a woman who stated another juror was heard to say during the trial, "My husband is just as jealous as Eggers, I expect the same thing will happen to me some day."

A judge denied the motion and on July 9, he was sentenced to die. By the time he was sent to San Quentin Prison he was described as a "wife butcher" by the press.

In August, Dorothy Eggers' estate worth $5000 was left to her only heir, her mother, Mary Elizabeth Lee.

Arthur Eggers' execution was slated for February, but it was not carried out until October 16, 1947. He went to his death denying he beheaded Dorothy and hid her body. He said, "Shot her I may have, but I never cut her up."

His body was claimed by his sister, Etta.

In December 1948, a bullet-riddled skull was found in the hills north of Indio, a few days later an 11-year-old boy found a lower jaw in another canyon a mile away. Also found were a pair of overalls with what appeared to be blood stains. Pieces of vertebrae along with other small human bones were scattered in the area. At the scene were guns shells, not all of them fired. The remains were turned over to a pathologist to determine if they belonged to Dorothy Eggers. It wasn't her.

In September 1954, another skull was found in Eaton Canyon. An autopsy surgeon examined it and compared it to photographs of Dorothy and he concluded it was not the same person.

Dorothy's missing head and hands were never found.

Arthur Eggers is led from the mortuary by his attorney after viewing the headless, armless torso

Source - Lindsay Gazette

Eggers house (above)
Detectives dig in the back yard of the house in an effort to
locate the victim's head and hands
Source - Lindsay Gazette

**Eggers family in happier times (above)
Dorothy & Arthur Eggers**

Source - Lindsay Gazette

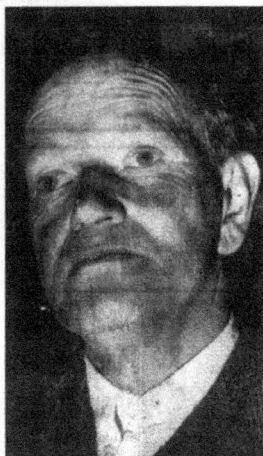

Eggers shows police how he disposed of his wife's head (left)

Eggers with attorney when convicted of 1st degree murder

Source - Linday Gazette

THIS BOX STARTED IT ALL

BRIDGETON, NEW JERSEY OCTOBER 20, 1904

Frank Rasinger's beautiful wife Elizabeth was dead. He was the one that found her inside their home on the Shiloh Turnpike, with the gun lying across her arms. She'd been shot through the heart while she stood at the ironing board. After examining the body, the coroner laid to rest any suspicion she committed suicide, since for good measure, another bullet was put in her side.

Convinced they missed something Constable Woodruff along with the coroner returned to the scene of the crime. They brought only one thing back, the clothes Frank Rasinger was wearing the day he found his murdered wife, all except his overalls which mysteriously disappeared.

They questioned Everett Shephard, an 11-year-old boy who worked on the farm. He was not there when the crime was committed or when the body was found. Normally he would not be gone during those afternoon hours when it was believed the murder took place. He told officials he went to the rear of the property, about half a mile away to pick hickory nuts. Mr. Rasinger gave him permission to do this, despite the fact there was considerable work to be done in the yard and house. When he returned at 3 p.m. he saw Frank Rasinger accompanied by the town doctor. Then he learned that Lizzie Rasinger was dead.

But before we get any further into the story of who killed the young housewife, we should explore what might have been the cause for such an inexplicable act of brutality.

It all started with Archibald Shimp Lupton, a mail carrier on the rural route known as the Shiloh Turnpike. As a joke he painted a 13 on the mailbox in front of the farm where the Rasingers moved into. The number became official as the address for the place.

Then came the day when Lizzie Rasinger was killed in cold blood with a shotgun.

Since that time strange happenings were reported on the property. One tenant after another left, all telling stories of strange noises, sounds of imaginary quarrels and a feeling of unbearable loneliness pervading the place.

Was it Lizzie Rasinger's fate to be murdered or was it the "hoodoo" cast on the property after the 13 was designated to mark the property?

Twenty-five years later, in the spring of 1929, Walter Minch moved into the house where Lizzie was killed in cold blood while standing at her ironing board. He ignored all the stories told about the farmhouse.

He did not have long to wait to start feeling the bad luck that perched on the unfortunately numbered mailbox.

The first incident was when Walter Morrison, 18, and two accomplices stole a truck and farming equipment from Mr. Minch. They were indicted for the crime; however it turned out that two years before Morrison's mother was killed by her own brother, William Workheiser.

Walter Morrison was the state's principal witness; however he turned out to be a poor one after changing his story four different times, despite the fact this trial involved the death of his mother.

Originally he said his uncle struck her over the head with a pipe and killed her. Then he took her body out into the country in the automobile.

Workheiser told police he fought with his sister, but hadn't struck her. She fell out of the car and her head hit the road. She died three days later. Due to the inconsistency in the stories the grand jury failed to return a true bill against Workheiser.

The mysterious death of Mary Morrison at the hands of her brother seemed a strange foreshadowing of what occurred on August, 6, 1929.

Mrs. Minch, 55, was crossing the street when an automobile struck her. A later autopsy found she died from internal injuries and a fractured skull. The driver was a 21-year-old named Walter Lively, and he was facing a charge of manslaughter.

Within two weeks of the tragedy, all were pointing to the trail of misfortune that plagued those who lived at the farmhouse. No doubt the structure had a "haunt" on it.

The first one that thought of it as the reason for his ill fortune was Walter Minch.

But it appears Mr. Minch was practical, because despite the hoodoo curse on his farm, within less than a year he tied the knot with Mathilda Laning. She was six years younger than him, but she died six years later, and Mr. Minch was once more a widower.

Then in 1938 he married a third time. Her name was Claudine DuBois, who did outlive him by nine years. More than likely they relocated from the house on the Shiloh Turnpike.

Years afterwards it became known the carrier who numbered the mailbox, suffered his own misfortunes and lost all but his job.

But let's resume the story of the unfortunate Lizzie Rasinger, who seems to be the first victim of the "hoodoo" haunting the farmhouse.

It turned out she was killed by a charge of heavy bird shot fired a few feet into her left side just below the heart. The shot was fired from her husband's double-barrel shotgun which had been standing in a corner of the kitchen. Each barrel contained a charge of No. 4 shot.

Her 10 month old baby had upset its cradle and crawled across the floor, staining it hands with its mother's blood. When found the child held its arms around her neck and was crying piteously.

There was every indication of a desperate struggle in the house, and it seemed she was shot down when she tried to flee from the house.

Strangely enough Rasinger insisted his wife had been sexually assaulted before being killed. Her body was bruised and her clothes torn, however the pathologist confirmed she had not been raped prior to death.

By October 21, at the inquest into Lizzie's death Frank Rasinger had become the prime suspect and he was arrested. Pending evidence against him, he was not charged with murder and was just held as a witness.

Ananias Wentzell mother of Mrs. Rasinger, took care of her daughter's child, and refused to believe her son-in-law killed Lizzie. Of her ten children she said her daughter was the happiest, and the couple seemed to be content.

But perhaps the difficulties started earlier. The couple married on May 19, 1900, and Lizzie bore a stillborn son two months later on July 15. After this she had two more children, another born dead, and the third dying in infancy. The only one to survive was their son Paul, age 10 months.

Did they marry because of her first pregnancy? Perhaps one of them if left to follow their heart would not have married.

The prosecutor and the coroner took measurements of the exact distance between the kitchen where the victim was killed, and the place in the carriage house where Mr. Rasinger claimed he was sorting potatoes. The distance was sixty-one feet. The kitchen windows were open and the outbuilding where Frank Rasinger worked had various cracks which should have made the shots clearly audible to him.

He said he heard the shots sound far away and even mistook them for a door slamming. Everett Shepherd who was a quarter of a mile away heard the shots distinctly. The distance was so close that if the victim had been accosted, all she had to do was to call out for her husband. There was also a discrepancy in Rasinger's statement that he was working in the carriage house for ninety minutes, however he had sorted only one bushel which normally took fifteen minutes.

At Lizzie Rasinger's funeral her husband, in custody of the authorities, showed much grief. Afterwards he was returned to jail. The following day he was formally charged with the murder of his wife. The authorities said that whoever shot Mrs. Rasinger was not a stranger. He had a thorough knowledge of the house and knew how to find their way about.

Both the Wentzell and Rasinger families were distraught, and wondered who could have committed this crime.

The townspeople feared a killer roamed the countryside killing innocent women, but in the truth the murderer was much closer. Frank Rasinger finally confessed. He said his wife refused him certain requests of a private nature and that he lost his temper and shot her.

As tragic as the death of the young wife was, the motive was the strangest of all. Rasinger declared a murderous passion smoldered inside of him. The couple had many quarrels since the birth of their child 10 months before. Later he said he couldn't account for his outburst or what drove him to commit the act.

It seemed that Lizzie Rasinger found it difficult to have sex with her husband. She confided as such to her neighbors, and said it caused great difficulties between them. She declared she would end her life rather than again "undergo marital obligations". Her repulse of her husband while she was working in the kitchen led to the murder. Maybe the heartbreak of losing three children was too much for Lizzie Rasinger to endure, and she feared another pregnancy where she might lose another child.

However within a few hours, the story was changed when the reason for the quarrels between the couple stemmed from jealousy. It seemed that Frank Rasinger was involved with another woman.

Justice Hall issued the warrant for Rasinger's arrest, and based on this new allegation he visited Seeley a village eight miles from the Bridgton, where the woman in question lived. Apparently nothing came of the visit, for it was never mentioned again.

A few days later, Frank Rasinger added details to his confession which made his wife's death all the more pitiable.

"What I said about Lizzie and me not getting along well is true, and also about Everett Shepard going for hickory nuts and me entering the house and being repulsed by my wife. But I did not shoot her right then. I was determined to make her submit to me, and I overpowered her, though she fought hard. Then she grabbed my gun, which was standing in the corner, and drove me from the house. I knew the gun wasn't loaded, but I went."

"I stood outside and watched her fix up the furniture which we had upset, and return to her ironing. She was crying all the time. I don't know what was the matter with me, but I was so mad I couldn't think right. I went to the front door and crept into the sitting room. Lizzie didn't hear me, and I took the gun from behind the door and got a shell from the cupboard."

"I had just about got the gun loaded when my wife turned around and saw me. She screamed, threw the apron over her head, and I fired. She dropped where she stood and I unloaded the gun and put another shell in the same barrel. Then I turned to my wife, who was still alive, and fearing she would tell on me if she lived, I placed the muzzle of the gun to the first wound and fired again, killing her instantly."

After these details were known the feeling of the people was intense. In the neighborhood of the Rasinger farm, the Seventh Day Baptist sect was strong; there was an open discussion that if the law failed in this case there would be violence.

The trial started January, 1905, and ended with the prompt conviction of Frank Rasinger for the murder of his wife. He was to be hung in February.

Benjamin Rasinger, Frank's father attempted to hang himself at his farm on the Marlboro Road. He was found just as he kicked a soapbox out from beneath him by a farmhand who cut him down.

A gallows was quickly erected outside the county jail within hearing distance of where Frank Rasinger sat in his cell. The hammer blows couldn't be ignored, and the court ordered a screen enclosure to shield the place of execution from public view. That did not stop the crowds from gathering.

On February 15, at 10 a.m. Frank Rasinger was led to the gallows. When Sheriff Diament pulled the lever, the body dropped through the opening and broke the rope. His head struck on the cross beam of the scaffold. One hundred witnesses were horrified as four men ran up and grasped the rope at the open trap. They held the prisoner suspended for nine minute until the doctor pronounced him dead. Later it was determined his neck was broken by the first drop.

A piece of the rope was put on display at Weston's, a local store.

Mail carrier in front of "hoodooed" mailbox on Shiloh Turnpike (above) c.1929 Bridgton, NJ c.1920s
Source - The Blockton Enterprise

TROUBLE

IN

TEXAS

PERRYTON, TEXAS FEBRUARY 19, 1939

Like most discoveries of this type, it was sheer chance, luck or perhaps the spirits of those left to rot in their secret graves, to be fed upon by buzzards and coyotes that steer the living to discover them.

It all started on a windswept day in when Lloyd Davis, a WPA worker making a mineral survey on the Merydith Ranch stumbled on a skull and part of a skeleton. His discovery revived a seven year old mystery.

On May 31, 1932, J. M. Cone Jr., 10, and his brother, Vernon, 6, disappeared. The next day their father, Jean M. Cone, a radiator repairman, was found shot twice in the chest inside the garage of his home. His death was ruled a suicide despite unusual circumstances surrounding the event.

What happened to the boys, and why would his father kill himself, even though the family believed he would not have committed this act of self destruction, remained a mystery in the town of Perryton until 1936.

It was then that Warden J. W. Lewis of the Oregon State Penitentiary sent Sheriff Talley a letter detailing where two convicts Claude and Elmer "Fats" Tenison, who once lived in Perryton, confessed to the murder of the Cone boys. They were serving an 18 year stretch for robbing the Dairymen's Bank at Redmond.

Claude Tenison had served prison time in Nebraska and Texas on other charges before this.

According to them, they shot Jean Cone when he paid them only $250, a quarter of what he promised them for their bloody work. They told authorities that each of them had shot a child in the back, and buried them about 25 miles southeast of Perryton at Wolf Creek.

Sheriff Talley discounted the confession, and said "those old boys want to get out of prison and get a trip back home."

The discovery of the bones corresponded to where the convicts said they committed the crime, and Perryton officials reopened the investigation.

The parole board in Oregon brought the brothers back in to be questioned, and they repeated their prior story. They said Cone wanted to kill his sons because he "had too many kids and didn't want to take them with him when he was going to run off with another woman."

The bones were sent to the state police in Austin in order to identify them. The examination found the skeleton belonged to a male from 8 to 13 years of age, which corresponded with the oldest boy.

By May 1939, officials said they would probably ask for indictments and take the brothers to Texas after they completed their sentences in Oregon. These plans were never acted upon, and it wasn't until January, 1945 when Sheriff Bill Lance took his oath of office that the case was seriously investigated.

Authorities started with retracing the steps J.M. Cone took the last time the boys were seen. He took them on a drive, stopping at a local service station where he bought Vernon a soda pop. They were then seen turning south on the Ochiltree Lipscomb County line heading towards Wolf Creek.

Nellie Cone in a statement made to the police said she went to bed that night pondering on the whereabouts of her husband and children. At 3 a.m. she heard someone enter the house. She turned on a light in time to see a man open the bathroom door and then heard him leave the house. She did not awaken her other children who were asleep, but she could not deny the terrible premonition that something bad was going to happen to Jean. Then between 5 to 6 a.m. she heard what sounded like a shot coming from the garage.

She woke up Alvia, her teenage stepson, and asked him to help her with the weekly wash, knowing these things were stored in the garage. He returned right away telling her both doors in the garage were locked. The larger one where the car would enter was locked from inside, and the smaller one on the side had a new padlock on it.

Alvie finally opened the door and found his father lying on the wash bench, He said, "He looked pale and sick. I asked him what was the matter and he replied, 'Nothing I'm all right.'"

The family car was inside the garage but the keys were missing. Alvie told his brother Floyd to make sure none of the other family members went into the garage, and then he ran to the neighbor's house and asked to borrow their car. He rushed to the home of Dr. Brewer asking him to come to his house. En route back he saw a friend of his father's named Fred Chor. He picked him up and they headed back, and as they pulled into the driveway they heard the report of a pistol and saw the flame from a gun coming from inside the garage.

Moments later Dr. Brewer arrived. He found a pistol on Jean Cone's lap and he put it in his pocket. He told Alvie and Fred to get an ambulance and notify the police. Jean Cone was shot twice in the chest. He died fifteen minutes after arriving at the Perryton hospital.

While searching Jean Cone's clothes, officers found a letter. Relatives said it was in his handwriting. It read, "Nellie, for everything and everyone concerned I think this is the best thing to do. I am not guilty of Reta's condition as you accused me of, but this will relieve you of lots of responsibility. Try to be as good to mine as I have been to yours..."

There was no mention of the fate of either boy, although other notes were left for Alvie, and his daughter Elmyra.

Officers learned that Cone's stepdaughter Reta Hammonds, 19, was pregnant, and she later made a statement declaring her step-father was responsible.

Police found a freshly made bullet hole in the garage wall about five and half feet above the floor, indicating the gun had been fired from someone lying on the floor. Was this done by a muscle contraction from the dying man?

After the discovery of Jean Cone in the garage, the family along with citizens made every effort to find the boys. They traced Cone's auto over the county line road south of Wolf Creek on the Merydith Ranch. They found tire tracks matching the tread of Cone's car. They also came across bare-footed tracks which matched those of the boys and prints that matched the soles of their father's boots.

There was evidence that Cone turned his car around at the swollen creek since it had been raining for several days, and headed back to Perryton. Officers confirmed that Cone could not have crossed the creek or traveled on the creek road since it was inundated.

However sand was found inside Cone's shirt pocket and trouser cuffs matching the sand at Wolf' Creek.

In 1945, the family expressed doubts regarding the findings of the inquest which ruled Jean Cone's death a suicide. They said testimony was not taken by the officers at the scene, nor from Reta, Cone's stepdaughter.

Who fired the shot seen by Alvie Cone when he returned home? Could a man shoot himself twice in the chest? The biggest mystery of all is why he did not mention what happened to his two sons.

These questions remained unanswered and the family was not happy with the verdict.

Fred Chor said his friend had been involved with another woman, and was infatuated with her. He believed that Cone planned to run away with her, and that Cone told him once, "The first of June you'll be surprised. I'll be gone, or something like that."

W. A. Cone, brother of Jean testified at the inquest that his brother never hinted at suicide but he recalled a talk they had the year before, where his brother said, "If I am ever killed, I will not have done it, but it will be with my own gun."

Sheriff Sid Talley who held the office for 36 years and was in charge of the original investigation, believed Cone killed his sons and then himself. He told a newspaper reporter, "Jean Cone was seen along Beaver River by a storekeeper, the afternoon of May 30, 1932, sweating, tired and non-talkative." He said his belief was that Cone killed and buried the boys along the river's drifting sand dunes. According to him, Harry Cone, Jean's father, came to his office after inspecting the family graveyard along the Beaver River and said, "Jean put the children where he wanted them. Let's drop the case."

Was this the secret burial spot of the boys, inside the family plot?

Officers recalled that Elmer "Fats" Tenison came with them on June 1, 1932 when they traced Cone's car to Wolf Creek. They knew his brother Claude Tenison was in Canadian, about 54 miles south of Perryton. The night the boys disappeared he was in the company of the woman Jean Cone was having an affair with. The car they were using that night was reported stolen, and was never located. The policemen said that in later years, this woman followed the Tenison brothers out to Oregon.

Fats Tenison enjoyed a reputation as a "bootlegger and tin-horn gambler". Claude though was the hardened one having done prison time for car stealing, liquor violations and breaking out of jail.

Now in 1945, perhaps because they were closer to ending their sentence, when several police and a judge went to Oregon to interview the pair, Claude refused to talk, and Fats was the opposite, almost eager to discuss the murders.

The police based their disbelief of the confession because they described something that was impossible during those days the murder was committed, which was taking the creek route in order to dispose of the bodies.

There was also controversy if indeed the skull found belonged to one of the Cone boys since the area was the site of where a wagon train was destroyed by Indians and the occupants killed prior to 1886.

In the end the known facts were that Jean Cone was in the garage with all the doors locked from the outside. The car was there, but missing the keys. When Nellie Cone and Alvie found Jean they saw no wounds or a gun.

159

There was the shot that Nellie Cone heard about 3 a.m., and then another shot seen when the garage was opened. A pistol was found in Jean Cone's lap, but who shot the bullet into the wall?

There was no arguing the fact the boys were missing after leaving with their father, and Cone's remarks about dying by his own gun deepened the mystery even further.

The convicts' stories sounded convincing except that where they said they buried the bodies was impossible to access because of high water.

Dr. Brewer who first examined Jean Cone said either of the shots could have been fatal. Could he have shot himself a second time?

The background on the family gave no warning this tragedy would occur.

Nellie Cone became the widow of John Hammonds in 1913. She was left with four children, newborn Reta, another daughter Jimmie and two sons, Floyd and Johnson. She married Jean Cone in 1915. They went on to have their own children.

In the 1930 census, J. M. Cone and his wife Nellie lived on Wyman Street in Perryton with Jimmie Hammonds, 24, Floyd Hammonds 22, Johnson Hammonds, 20, Reta Hammonds 17, Alvia Cone, 14, Elmyra Cone, 11, Jean Cone Jr. 11 and Vernon age 4.

However something had fractured in their 17-year marriage. Nellie Cone suspected her husband of impregnating his stepdaughter, and he was having an affair with another woman.

If there was one person who perhaps could have answered every question was the unknown woman Cone was involved with, and who went on to join the Tenison brothers in Oregon. Was she the one that fed the convicts the information of where the boys were buried, because Jean Cone confided this secret to her?

Until this day, where the boys were interred, and why and who ended their life remains a mystery.

Jean & Nellie Cone
(above)

Jean & Vernon Cone
(left)

Claude & Elmer "Fats" Tenison
both confessed to the murder of
the Cone boys

UNCLE BILLY

AND THE AXE

BADLANDS, MONTANA, LATE 19TH CENTURY

Buffalo Bill Cody was famous for his exploits as a soldier and a scout. One day he traveled with a party of eighteen men through the Black Hills in Montana. Off in the distance they saw horsemen approaching, and once they were close they saw it was seven, heavily armed horsemen.

Cody stopped them and inquired where there was a good place to camp. Then after getting a better look at one of them he asked, "What are you doing here, Frank?" The man looked at him with wary eyes until Cody identified himself. They decided to camp out together, and that night Cody's 14-year-old cook named Billy Royce prepared a meal of venison and wild turkey. Billy was the son of an Irish doorkeeper at the White House when Lincoln was president.

Many years later, Billy Royce and Frank James once more crossed path on the streets of Cement, Oklahoma. They struck up an acquaintance and it was during one of their frequent conversations that James told Royce a story.

He described that after the Kearney bank robbery, the authorities gave chase and the gang traveled deep into the Keechi Hills beyond the settlement of the Indian Territory. Frank and his brother Jesse James along with the Ford boys took refuge at a spring near the foot of what was known as Buzzard Roost Mountain. This spot was on a 160-acre homestead belonging to Belle Hedlund. She had recently drilled an oil well that produced 100 barrels a day.

The gang filled two copper kettles with $12,000 worth of loot. They drew a map and clues leading to where they were buried. The story ended with Frank James asking Royce for help. He had found some clues, but not the actual tree where the treasure was buried.

Eventually Billy Royce found the tree on his farm, and he was eager to tell Frank James of his discovery, however Frank learned of it before Royce saw him. That night Frank James, with another man dug up the kettle and left with the gold. Throughout the years, especially after James' death in 1915, many searched for the second kettle of gold.

For all those years, Royce persisted, dotting his homestead with holes, hoping to find the lost treasure.

Then on a cold, winter day in January, 1935, Roy and Lois Alexander came to see their mother at the three-room shack where she lived with her new husband, Charles William Royce, known in the community as "Uncle Billy".

Ethel Leta Royce, 45, had married Royce, who was 23 years her senior, only a few weeks before. She had kept house for him for eight months before that.

When her sons asked him where she was, he was evasive and then said something very queer, which was that a "Dutchman came by and offered her $1 a day and board to go to Mexico and cook for him." Then they found her coat and hat in a closet and their next stop was to see Undersheriff

Harp at Anadarko who launched a search for the missing woman

Harp went to the farm but found no trace of Leta Royce. The search became difficult because Uncle Billy had dug dozens of pits on the farm.

The undersheriff returned to the farm with a search warrant in hand. Royce was gone and the house was locked. He broke in and within seconds he knew something dreadful happened to Mrs. Royce. A bloody axe was in the kitchen, and he followed a blood trail that meandered about 50 feet out to the hen house. This was also locked, but he forced his way inside the small building which measured about 18 feet by 8 feet. He pulled off a cloth that covered the earthen floor, and started to dig through the loosely-packed dirt.

Only three inches down his shovel hit what was left of Mrs. Royce. She was dressed in her pajama house dress, and her mutilated remains were jammed into a grave measuring less than five feet long. The whole top of her head had been taken off by the blade of the axe.

This was the second tragedy Leta's seven children suffered, since their father O. S. Alexander committed suicide in 1933.

Deputy Ruff was called in, and when authorities questioned Royce they realized he was partially deaf and showed signs of being mentally unbalanced. He admitted to having a fight with his wife and that she lunged at him with a butcher knife. The old man insisted he had defended himself and that he gave the "Dutchman" $5 to take her body away; however he couldn't recall what the man's name was, or what he looked like.

Royce offered no resistance when he was arrested, even though he was known to carry a .38-caliber pistol.

The old man implicated his former wife Carrie Royce and Reed Norris, 27. He said Reed buried the body, and Carrie urged him to kill his new wife. They were both arrested at the same home in Norge, Oklahoma. They had witnesses who provided alibis for their whereabouts the night Leta Royce was butchered.

Reed Norris' relationship varies; in some instances the newspapers describe him as Carrie Royce's son-in-law or married to one of her nieces, or as her son by another marriage. In some stories he was Royce's son by a previous relationship. The fact that both Carrie and Reed were residing in the same household points to a familial connection between them.

The police found out that during those days when his dead wife lay rotting under the henhouse Uncle Billy told neighbors who came inquiring after her that he offered a "Dutchman" $5 take his wife away since they often fought.

The old man told police he bought the farm because the notorious Frank James, member of the outlaw gang, who owned a homestead nearby told him there was a possibility of buried loot on the grounds. According to a book, *Coronado's Children* published in 1930, there was a treasure worth $2 million dollars secreted in the area.

Officers were trying to find a copy of an alleged pre-nuptial contract between Royce and Leta, which seemed to point for a motive for the killing. It was found on file with the office of the county clerk in Anadarko. In addition to the farm, he also owned oil lands near Cyril, and acreage at Norge, and all of them were included in the agreement. Everything was willed to the new Mrs. Royce.

Police also found yellowed newspaper clippings that attested to the fact that Royce had a part in recovering $6,000 worth of loot taken by the James gang when they robbed a bank at Carney, Missouri.

Towards the end of January, William Royce was committed to the state asylum after a hearing found him to be insane. The murder charges against him were dropped. He died in 1950, outliving Carrie Royce who died in 1940. None were prosecuted for the crime.

And what about Uncle Billy's land, which cost a woman her life. One has to wonder who ended up with it, and possibly a treasure in stolen gold.

James Gangs Buried Gold has Never Been Found

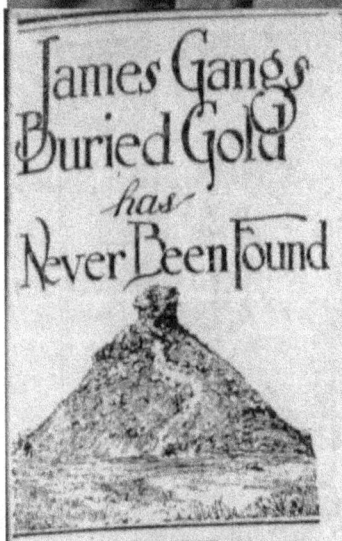

Frank James in later years (above)

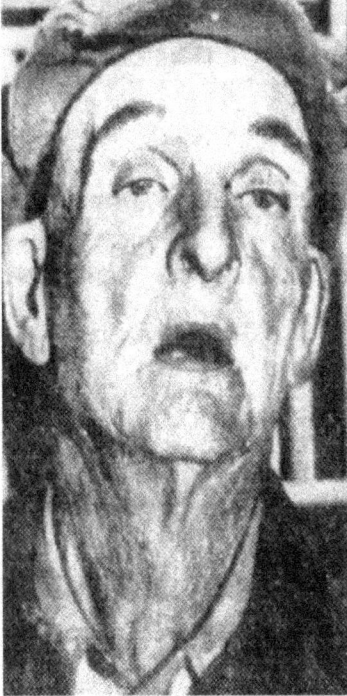

View from top
of Buzzard's
Roost (above)

William "Billy"
Royce c.1935

*Source - The Mangum
Daily Star Sun*

MISTRESS OF THE TOMBSTONES

St. Bernard Parish, Louisiana 1842

In 1842, Louis E. Collins a native of Ireland, and Mr. Eugene Musson met on the grounds of the Treme Plantation for a duel. It was over rumors circulating about illegal banking activity. Collins was shot through the body. The doctor feared it was fatal, but he recovered and died in 1890.

Three years later, two Creole men once more stood under the shade of large oak trees on the Treme Plantation. Despite the early morning hour, the day radiated humid heat. Their names were Judge Gilbert Leonard and Philip Toca, Esquire, and they met to settle a disagreement using the Code, which was a duel. The weapons used were double barrel shotguns, and they paced 150 feet away from each other, and then swung around to shoot at the count of three.

The first shot harmed neither man, but the second shot wounded Leonard, who was struck on the left breast breaking his rib. It was not considered a mortal wound on that day. However this proved to be a mistaken assessment because Leonard died on April 8.

Gilbert Leonard, 46, was a handsome and popular man, but known to settle arguments via duels. A few months before he challenged and killed a Creole named Descommes Vaux.

In May 1859, the body of F. A. Brown, a Frenchman was found on the grounds of the Treme Plantation. He committed suicide by taking an overdose of arsenic. In a diary found in his pocket it told that he was the first officer of the ship *Baden* which sailed from Havre. In April, he fell through the "sister hatchway" and landed on the ballast. Once in New Orleans he went to the Marine Hospital at Algiers seeking medical care, however he was rejected. The next day he took his life. He was only 25 years old.

This baptism by blood, foreshadowed violent death that was to haunt the owners of this piece of land for years to come. The years slipped by and the plantation situated on the right bank of Bayou Terre-aux-Boeufs was reduced in size until only 14 acres were left.

A dive into records between the days when duels were fought on the Treme Plantation, and the grisly end of the last owner Dorothy Robinson reveals a history of high strangeness. It centers on the property that in the 1950s became a pet cemetery drawing visitors from all over the South. However it's not the land only, but Dorothy herself and the biography of her family which is replete with bizarre events.

In 1913, Grace Agnes Matt married John "Jack" Thompson who hailed from Kansas City, Missouri. She was a stenographer at the Detention Home and he was a probation officer at the juvenile court.

Six years later the marriage had soured and Grace ran off with her lover Arthur Wynne. Once divorced from Jack, they married and a daughter, Dorothy was born to them in 1924.

Perhaps Grace was Jack Thompson's one true love, because even though he married Mary L. Thompson in the intervening years, he continued to see his ex-wife Grace in Oklahoma City.

In 1931, Jack convinced Grace to return to Kansas City and she divorced Arthur Wynne.

As to Grace's ambitions, perhaps they were not as romantic. In 1929, the stock market crash damaged the economy. In 1930, she lived in a boarding house on 7th Street in Oklahoma City, with her daughter and husband. Arthur was 10 years older than her, and he was employed as a tanner. Compared to her ex-husband he came in a distant second, at least when it came to economic security. One could easily believe that Grace was scolding herself soundly for having left Jack.

Thompson's star was ascending, and he was described as "an influential politician, a successful operator of slot machines and a man of considerable means."

Politically he hitched his wagon to Tom Pendergast, better known as "Boss Tom" of Kansas City, who through his mafia connections operated all the illegal activities born of Prohibition. He rigged elections, made sure to grease police palms, ran brothels, gambling houses and of course sold illegal hooch.

Jack Thompson set up his ex-wife, now mistress, in the swanky Pickwick Hotel, lavishing her with gifts, and visiting her every day to eat lunch. Dorothy took to calling him "Daddy Jack" and in adulthood used his surname.

Three years later, Grace had grown tired of being the "other woman", or perhaps Jack told her there was only one way they could marry again. So on an autumn night in 1934, Grace waited outside Jack's home at 6700 Montgall Avenue and shot the current Mrs. Thompson, several times, injuring her critically.

According to Grace she went to the home to try to convince Mrs. Thompson to leave her husband, and the fight escalated. She had no choice but to shoot the woman in "self defense."

Later the authorities verified that Grace filed a petition to regain her ex-husband's surname just two weeks before the shooting.

Grace told police that Thompson had sought her out in Oklahoma City six years before, trying to convince her to return to Kansas City. Three years later she returned with him based on Thompson's promise they could remarry once they divorced their respective spouses. Three more years passed, and Grace lived at Pickwick Hotel, supported monetarily by Jack, but no closer to regaining her title of "Mrs. Thompson."

She told authorities she had spoken to the current Mrs. Thompson several times over the phone, but the woman just laughed at her and hung up. She felt forced to confront her rival in person. The .25 caliber pistol she used was one she habitually carried in her handbag.

Jack Thompson denied her entire story.

A few days later Mary Thompson died, and Grace was charged with first degree murder. Her mother Emma Matt came to Kansas City to accompany her daughter.

Two months later, Grace Wynne was adjudged insane by a jury in the probate court. The management of her affairs was given to her mother. She was taken to St. Joseph hospital. The murder charge was dismissed.

It did not take long for the doctors at the asylum to realize Grace Wynne was not insane. Mrs. Matt asked for her daughter to be released, however this move was a two-edged sword. A judge in the probate court stated he planned to put the prosecutor's office on notice and advise the criminal court.

A letter written by Dr. J. R. Bunch at the hospital read, "Mrs. Grace Wynne, white female, born October 20, 1890, height 5 feet 2 inches, weight 145 pounds, gray eyes, brown hair, residence, Pickwick Hotel, Kansas City, Missouri was committed to state hospital No. 2 by order of the Jackson County probate court November 27, 1934. This is to advise that we have found no evidence of insanity in the above named person and recommend that she be released from this hospital."

Six months after his wife's murder Jack Thompson resigned his position as Superintendent of Maintenance for the Park Department. He had not returned to work since the day of the shooting in September.

July, 1935, newspapers reported that Grace Wynne had disappeared from the state hospital. It seemed that Grace was paroled for a day to visit her sick mother, however she never returned to the hospital. When they called Mrs. Matt's home, her telephone had been disconnected. The sheriff immediately went to the house, but no one was there and a neighbor told them Mrs. Matt had paid him to take care of her lawn for two months, since she was going to "where it is cool."

Jack Thompson had moved to California by then.

Authorities realized that Grace Wynne had carefully planned her escape after giving up hope of escaping a murder trial in case she was declared sane. She had spoken to at least one attendant about the possibility of escaping.

Strangely, but perhaps not so strange considering Jack Thompson's connection, the papers reported that the probate courts appeared to have no further interest in the matter of locating Grace Wynne and returning her to Kansas City.

Like a moth to a flame, Jack Thompson could not stay away from Grace; however this was one time he came too close to the heat. In December, 1935, he arrived in New Orleans and checked into the Jung Hotel. He was found dead in his hotel room that night. According to Dr. C. Grene Cole, Orleans parish coroner he died from a complication of diseases due to natural causes. He was 41 years old.

There was no use denying the obvious fact that the state's principal witness in a murder case was dead.

In July, 1936, the law caught up to Grace's mother, Emma. She was sentenced to ten days in jail after refusing to reveal her daughter's whereabouts. She had returned to her home in Kansas City.

Grace hid in plain sight, but now using the name of Grace Thompson. She opened the Cottage Flower Shop on Freret St in New Orleans. She played the organ at Our Lady of Lourdes Church and published a gardening book titled "A Garden Book of Old New Orleans." None would believe she was a wanted woman.

It took another four years for the law to find Grace Wynne in Louisiana. It came in the form of a policewoman who traced her through a hymnal she published in 1939. She was arrested as a fugitive from Kansas City. She denied she was Grace Wynne and that she had ever been arrested. This did not stop her extradition to Missouri where she was convicted of second degree murder in 1942. She was to serve 15 years, however in 1944 the Missouri Supreme Court ordered a new trial for her based on a technicality.

According to Grace, the State of Missouri's witch hunt was tied to her relationship with Jack Thompson. She denied having any contact with Jack Thompson on the night he died, but contrary to the story he died from a heart attack, she said he was killed for his "hidden fortune" of nearly half-a-million dollars accumulated through illegal gambling activities. The money was never found.

Released on bond, Grace promptly fled to New Orleans, only to be brought back to Kansas City. During the extradition hearing in 1945 before Louisiana Gov. Jimmie Davis, her attorneys alleged that enemies of the corrupt Kansas City political machine were the ones bent on returning her to Missouri in order find Jack Thompson's fortune. The argument convinced Governor Davis who denied the extradition request.

Grace sold her flower shop in September 1946, and she, her mother and 21-year-old Dorothy moved to the Toca Plantation, a rural property in St. Bernard Parish. This property was once part of the Treme Plantation, but now it was just an abandoned sugarcane field surrounding a large, Edwardian house, built in 1909 by Sheriff Albert Estopinal Jr.

It was here that Grace brought to fruition plans she had for a pet cemetery.

Through 1947, the FBI still searched for Grace, but was unable to find her. Federal authorities in Kansas City occasionally made noises about bringing Grace back; however she never served time for the murder of Mary Thompson in 1934.

The cemetery had an ornate gate in the front. The first visible tomb was a large dog. This memorial was for Boots, a beloved member of the New Orleans Police K-9 Unit. Behind the dog, a cemetery blessing was on a large stone.

PET CEMETERY
FOUNDED IN 1946
BY GRACE MATT THOMPSON
DEAR FATHER
HEAR AND BLESS THY BEASTS
AND SINGING BIRDS
AND GUARD WITH TENDERNESS
SMALL THINGS WHO HAVE NO WORDS

By March 6, 1954, Grace stated she had 2 cats and 33 dogs buried on the property. In a 1965 ad she claimed, "a 9-year-old hen, a 30-year-old parrot, loads of monkeys and parakeets, 85 cats, and 800 dogs" found their final repose at E.E. Matt Plantation Garden in Toca Village.

Over the years, she teased the cemetery would expand to include pet boarding and human burials. Eventually she did board animals, but never made good on the human burials, as far as anyone knows that is.

Known also as the Azalea Original Pet Cemetery, eventually it drew pet owners from all over the South. At one point Grace said that 5,000 animals were buried there. Serita, the boa constrictor from the Tonight Show found her final resting place among the tropical flowers, but not before a choir sang "Goodnight, Irene."

The years crept forward, and along the way Dorothy met and married Logan Banks. They lived on the grounds of the cemetery.

It was Thanksgiving, November 26, 1970, when another Matt woman took matters into her hands and resolved it with a gun. The problem was Logan Banks, and Dorothy shot and killed him in the rear of the property. Grace confirmed her daughter's story that she acted in self defense. Banks was drunk and threatened to kill them with a large knife.

The local sheriff determined that Dorothy had no choice, and believed her story that a domestic squabble escalated into a dangerous situation.

Banks, 41, was an air force veteran and he left behind two children from another marriage.

The following year Grace transferred the ownership of the Azalea Pet Cemetery to her daughter.

On December 27, 1976, Dorothy married Donald E. Robinson a caretaker on the property. He was 12 years her junior. In July, 1978, she called police to report she found him dead on the front lawn of the property. He had been shot in the chest. No charges were filed against Dorothy or anyone else.

Grace Wynne died of natural cases in August, 1979. She was 88. She was buried in an unmarked grave at St. Bernard Memorial Gardens. By then Emma Matt had died as well.

Dorothy was now alone. Pat Newman who befriended Dorothy and later became executor of her estate described that after her mother's death, she never recovered. A few months later she hired Brandon Nodier, 26, to complete repairs on the property. His two-year-old son Brandon "Sonny Boy" Nodier accompanied him.

Dorothy did not know that Brandon suffered from his own troubled past. In 1961, his father, Germain Nodier, 36, was gunned down by George Bentzig, 61, a former mental patient. Brandon along with his five siblings was in the apartment when the murder took place, and one of them witnessed it. It was seven-year-old Brandon. The man lived in the same building, and rented an apartment from Nodier.

In his teenage years he started breaking into places and when he was 18 years old he was convicted of burglary.

Eventually he became a live in caretaker. Dorothy seemed to be the only one in the small town that did not know of his reputation as a conman.

December 1981, was a busy month for Brandon Nodier. On December 1, Dorothy signed a 99-year-lease for the cemetery to Brandon's Renovations, Inc. for $20 a month. On the 29th of the month he divorced his wife Bonnie.

What no one knew until a few months before her death was that Dorothy suffered from a "substance abuse dependency."

Perhaps this contributed to her decision to sign away the cemetery to Brandon and Bonnie Nodier, who were divorced but lived together. The price was $20,000; however a check was never found or cashed for the transaction.

In November, 1984, six months after she signed the contract Thompson filed a civil suit against the Nodiers, claiming they hoodwinked her.

Pat Newman described where the electrical power to Dorothy's home was cut several times, and she believed Brandon Nodier was the person responsible.

The case was scheduled for a pretrial conference on April 26, 1985, but mysteriously Dorothy disappeared on April 13. On May 2, fishermen snagged their line on something. The "something" turned out to be Dorothy, partially nude, wrapped in a chain. A garbage bag was tied around her head. The cause of death was suffocation and not drowning.

Authorities believed she was killed in the house and then dumped in the river.

After the discovery of Dorothy's body, no doubt the case was hindered by the squabbling of the two sheriffs' department who said they were not responsible for the investigation. It seemed that Dorothy was killed in St. Bernard Parish but her body was disposed of in Plaquemines Parish.

Suspicions abounded especially about Nodier, and witnesses came forward to complain of seeing Dorothy's ghost. The police could not find enough evidence to charge him with the crime though.

Police even used a psychic to crack the case.

In 1988, the judge ruled that Dorothy's heirs owned the property.

Pat Newman tried to sell the property, but couldn't even maintain it, since gardeners refused to work on the land, fearing their mowers would be damaged by the now hidden tombstones.

Hurricane Katrina hit the area badly in 2005, and further damaged the home and the grounds.

Throughout the years, police were often called to clear off delinquents and curiosity-seekers who stole many of the family valuables when the property was left abandoned.

Rumors swirled that Grace Wynne buried a fortune somewhere on the grounds, and those who came seeking Jack Thompson's loot came with metal detectors in hand. There were others who were happy enough to take one of the tombstones.

In 2009, residents in the area started coming to police with information about Nodier's involvement with Dorothy's death.

Around this time the only witness to the murder came forward and said he saw the crime take place, and also when Dorothy's body was disposed of. The witness said Nodier visited him in St. Tammany Prison several years afterwards and made veiled threats about the incident to insure his silence. The witness also tied Nodier to the murder of another woman.

On April 25, 2012, Brandon Nodier turned himself into police. By then his record included charges for burglary, drugs, aggravated assault and illegal weapon charges.

In 2014, he accepted a plea deal on his 2012 indictment for second-degree murder. It was for a reduced charge of manslaughter and he received a 10-year-prison sentence.

Foliage has swallowed The Azalea Original Pet Cemetery and vines have covered the ruins of the home Grace fled to with her mother and daughter so many years ago. Many have reported ghosts on the grounds.

Perhaps it is Dorothy, Grace and Emma existing in a world where the lawn is manicured and the house towers above the small tombstones. In this place, their own pets play with the all others laid to rest throughout the years. Here there is no need to flee, and it is their haven where none can trouble their peace.

Grace Thompson Wynne c.1935 when she escaped from St. Joseph's Hospital and below with her pet Jerry who died after 35 years and was buried in the pet cemetery c.1960s

Emma Matt comforting her daughter Grace during murder trial of Mary Thompson c.1935

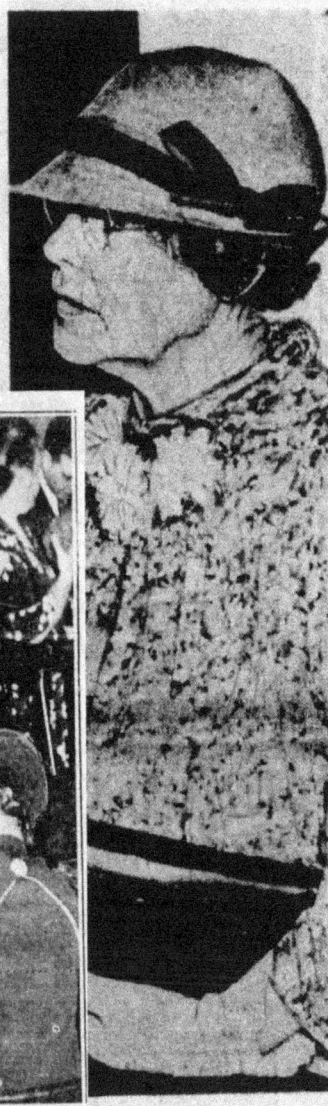

Jack Thompson behind the machine (above)
The Thompson house where Grace shot Mary
Thompson c.1934

Entrance gate to cemetery c.1976 Dorothy below with Brandon Nodier who would eventually murder her

St. Bernard Man Shot to Death

St. Bernard detectives were investigating the shooting death of Donald E. Robinson, 46, of Route 2, Box 216, St. Bernard, Friday night.

Detective Ray Spicuzza said the sheriff's department received a call from Doris Robinson, 58, who said she found her husband on the front lawn of their residence. He had been shot once in the chest.

Officers said the couple have lived in St. Bernard for the past two and a half years after coming here from Ohio.

An autopsy will be performed Saturday.

LOGAN BANKS' RITES PLANNED

Apparently Shot After Domestic Squabble

Funeral services will be conducted at 9 a.m. Wednesday for Logan R. Banks, 41, of Toca, who was shot to death after an apparent domestic squabble Thursday night at his residence, in the rear of the St. Bernard Pet Cemetery.

The Lamana-Panno-Fallo Funeral Home in St. Bernard is in charge of arrangements and services will be conducted at a chapel in the St. Bernard Memorial Gardens in Chalmette by the Rev. Wayne Crenshay of Bible Baptist Church in Chalmette.

Mr. Banks was apparently shot in self defense by his wife, 35-year-old Mrs. Dorothy Lou Banks, a sheriff's office spokesman said.

Notices about the death of Logan Banks & Donald Robinson

188

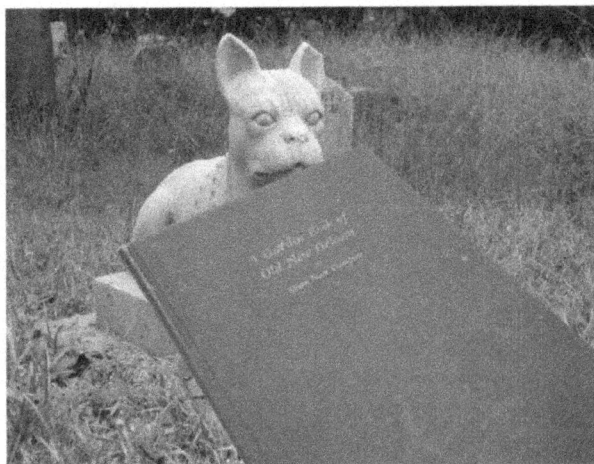

The pet cemetery became overgrown after the death of Dorothy

Brandon Nodier (above) c.2014
Pet cemetery open tomb damaged by the
passing of time and the elements.

Newspapers and Periodicals

Daily News; News Democrat; The Brooklyn Daily Eagle; The Meriden Daily Journal; Chicago Tribune; Des Moines Tribune; Greenville Daily Advocate; Los Angeles Record; Santa Ana Register; The Missoulian; The Los Angeles Times; The Pasadena Post; The Record; The Star Press; The Tampa Tribune; Oakland Tribune; Lindsay Gazette; The San Bernardino County; Intelligencer Journal; The York Dispatch; Lincoln Journal Star; The Decatur Herald; The San Francisco Examiner; Statesman Journal; The Boston Globe; The Tulsa Tribune; Wausau Daily Herald; New York Daily News; The Tampa Times; The Tampa Tribune; Courier Post; The Blocton Enterprise; Albany Democrat Herald; Amarillo Daily News; Corsicana Daily; The Evening; The Kansas City Star; The Mangum Daily Star; The Courier Journal; The Kansas City Star; The Opelousas Patriot; The Shreveport Journal; The Times Picayune; The Times Recorder; New York World; The Sacramento Union; The North East Sun; Omaha Daily Bee; Hemet News; The Record; Evening Independent; Lincoln County Leader; Enterprise; St. Joseph Gazette

www.ingramcontent.com/pod-product-compliance
Lightning Source LLC
Chambersburg PA
CBHW022107280326
41933CB00007B/287